# PRAISE FOR
# *THE ENTREPRENEUR'S BOOK*

"*The Entrepreneur's Book* is a fresh take on the question, 'What makes a successful entrepreneur?' Neil writes with honesty, humour and humanity about how his recovery from a life-threatening illness led him to a host of entrepreneurs and businesspeople and their experiences of successes (and sometimes failure!).

He concludes, perhaps surprisingly, that success comes not from answering the 'how' questions ('How do I write a business plan?') but from the 'why' questions ('Why purpose and not profit?' or 'Why will it be tough?'). He illustrates the why questions with a series of delightful stories and insights learned from the people he has encountered along the way.

I'd recommend this book as a 'must read' to anyone involved in running their own business and struggling to work out their best next step."

**Sir Tom Shebbeare,** Chairman, Virgin Start Up

"Wander round the 'business' section of your local bookstore, Amazon or wherever and you will quickly realise that, in the field of entrepreneurship and small business development, 'how-to' books are two a penny. *The Entrepreneur's Book* is refreshingly different. It addresses not the 'how' and 'what' of entrepreneurship but the 'why'. In a series of vignettes covering the full start-up and business development process, Neil Francis tells the stories of successful (and not-so-successful) entrepreneurs and draws on his own experience to reflect on the values, principles and emotions on which entrepreneurial action is based. In so doing, he highlights the importance of themes such as belief, purpose, values, love, compassion, peace, loneliness, luck, trust and perseverance in entrepreneurship as a world-shaping and world-changing activity. In asking 'why', not telling 'how', *The Entrepreneur's Book* is a refreshing, stimulating, thought-provoking and enjoyable guide to the changing face of entrepreneurship in the 21st century."

**Professor Richard T Harrison,** Chair of Entrepreneurship and Innovation and Director of the Compassionate Leadership Initiative, University of Edinburgh Business School

"It is refreshing to read a book where the human side of the word 'entrepreneur' is front and centre. All too often, today's media presents us with a skewed perspective on what being an entrepreneur is really all about. And it is not simply money ...

In this book, Neil Francis considers topics such as love and failure, not simply from an operational or functional narrative. No, Neil considers how these actually shape and form an entrepreneur on the long journey to success.

An insightful and honest 21st century read for anyone in and around the mercurial world of entrepreneurship."

**Jim Duffy MBE,** Co-Founder of Entrepreneurial Spark and Author of *Create Special*

"A book about entrepreneurship that gets to the heart of the matter – values, purpose, love and fear. Neil talks about the 'why', without which businesses (and books) become less about creating connection and value and more about the day-to-day job – and who wants one of those?"

**Amanda Hamilton,** Best-selling Author, Nutritionist & Health Activist, Entrepreneur

"One of the joys of working as a coach with CEOs is the range of decisions, opportunities, challenges and issues that are discussed. Usually the 'how' of the issue is diagnosed first, but it is essentially in the 'why' discussion where real value and insight is gained. It is of no real surprise to me then that *The Entrepreneur's Book* firmly establishes the 'why' as its backbone, making us think beyond the norm to stretch our thinking.

But it is in the storytelling where Neil Francis excels. His reflections on the entrepreneurs he has met and his xperience caddying for executive golfers is seductive, turning each round into a story, each story into a journey and each journey into a life lesson for entrepreneurs.

A fabulous uplifting read – a must for all budding, and experienced, entrepreneurs."

**George Hall,** Chairman, Vistage Group

"Understanding your 'why' is at the core of everything in life, including business. Through case studies and Neil's shared experience, this book will assist any entrepreneur to ensure their business stays on track."

**Russell Dalgleish,** Managing Partner,
Exolta Capital Partners

"Purpose and heart are foundational to any successful launch effort. In *The Entrepreneur's Book*, Neil lives the words he writes. He powerfully shares the wisdom and experience he has gained, in life and in business, to help this next generation of entrepreneurs succeed."

**Sanyin Siang,** CEO Coach
and Author of *The Launch Book*

Published by
**LID Publishing Limited**
The Record Hall, Studio 204,
16-16a Baldwins Gardens,
London EC1N 7RJ, UK

524 Broadway, 11th Floor, Suite 08-120,
New York, NY 10012, US

info@lidpublishing.com
www.lidpublishing.com

A member of:

**BPR**
Business Publishers Roundtable

**www.businesspublishersroundtable.com**

© Neil Francis, 2018
© LID Publishing Limited, 2018

Printed in the Czech Republic by Finidr

ISBN: 978-1-911498-81-0

Cover design: Caroline Li
Page design: Matthew Renaudin

# THE ENTREPRENEUR'S BOOK

**THE CRUCIAL 'WHY' QUESTIONS
THAT DETERMINE SUCCESS**

## NEIL FRANCIS

LONDON     NEW YORK     BOGOTA
MADRID     BARCELONA     BUENOS AIRES
MEXICO CITY     MONTERREY     SHANGHAI

# FOR OTHER TITLES
# IN THE SERIES...

CONCISE
SMALL
BOOKS:
BIG
IDEAS
ADVICE
LAB

---

---

Louise – well, that was an adventure!

Massive thanks and loads of love for everything you did
to help make this book become a reality.

# CONTENTS

# ACKNOWLEDGMENTS

Well, here it is, *The Entrepreneur's Book*. Yes, I wrote it, but boy have I had such so much help. So, huge thanks go to:

Bernie Petrie and Dougie West, who read the first draft of the manuscript.

Nicholas Hitimana, Ali Graham, Chris Wilkins, Abesh Thakur, Varun Nair and Simon Duffy for allowing me to share their stories. Also, all the many entrepreneurs I have met and the people I have caddied for.

Andy Hamilton, whose support made this book possible.

Gavin Cargill – you might recognize some of the aspects of the stories!

My long-suffering GPs, Dr Clare Doldon and Dr Gabriele Sulucci! It is down to them, and to many other brilliant people in the NHS who helped me to get to the stage, after my stroke, that I could write this book.

All the people at The North Berwick Golf Club – the starters, the caddies and the golfers.

The fantastic team at LID Publishing, especially Martin Liu, Sara Taheri, Liz Cooley, Matthew Renaudin and Hazel Bird.

Jack, Lucy and Sam – just love you all.

Finally, to my two daft golden retrievers – Dougal and Archie, whose walks on the beaches of North Berwick gave me the space to think and plan the book!

# INTRODUCTION
## THE UNDERTAKER

It all started with the undertaker, George.

You see, there was no plan to write a second book. But you know how these things go – one little event is the spark that takes you on a completely new adventure in your life.

My spark happened on the golf course when I caddied for George from Chicago. The time I spent with him led me to write the book you are currently holding in your hand (or reading on your tablet). However, before I tell you what that spark was, I think I should explain how I ended up caddying for George in the first place.

You see, 12 years ago I was a successful entrepreneur. In 1996, I was the co-founder and CEO of an internet company, Company Net, based in Edinburgh. My company led global internet projects with some of the top 100 international companies (for example, BP, The Coca-Cola Company, Disney and Microsoft). I grew Company Net to a point where it was bought by one of our major clients because we were doing so much work for them, and then, two years later, I organized a team to help me buy it back when the client was bought themselves by BP.

And then, at the age of 41, on 19 October 2006, I had a significant stroke and my life hit the pause button. My time as a CEO finished that day. The doctors told me that my stroke had been caused by a blood clot in my leg (a deep vein thrombosis) that I had developed during a flight to Boston, in the US, for business.

For about a year after the stroke, I couldn't effectively communicate. Words that were in my mind just wouldn't come out, even though I knew what I wanted to say. Also, for a while, my memory was incredibly poor. Something that had occurred an hour previously could have happened a year ago, or vice versa. I felt very confused and highly emotional. I had difficulty expressing my thoughts, feelings and emotions clearly. And trying to focus on more than one thing at a time was just impossible!

It was probably about 18 months after my stroke when my neuropsychologist told me that, because of the effects of the stroke, I would never be able to be a CEO again. I had to acknowledge that what I had thought was going to be a temporary pause was in fact going to be a full stop.

So, what on earth was I going to do? Well, about two years after my stroke, my wife and I watched a TV programme about the caddies at Scotland's Old Course, St Andrews, and afterwards my wife suggested that maybe I should think about caddying. She felt it would keep me fit and give me the opportunity to meet the types of people I'd previously worked with. She knew I would be able to relate to them and that it would be good for my confidence.

I'd always loved golf and was a member of a famous and historic club, North Berwick Golf Club, located about 25 miles outside Edinburgh. It attracts thousands of visitors each year. And so, I started caddying, and over the next three years I caddied for doctors, lawyers, judges, pilots, venture capitalists, millionaires, billionaires, sports champions, bankers, truck drivers, politicians, entrepreneurs, investment managers, professors, senators, estate agents, brokers and CEOs – from all sorts of locations around the world.

It was caddying for these people that eventually inspired me to write my first book, *Changing Course*, about starting again in life. The book was based on my experiences of being a CEO, stroke survivor and caddie. I eventually secured a publishing deal and the book hit the shelves in September 2013.

But, crucially, during this time I gained something even better than a publishing deal. Through conversations with the people I was caddying for, I began to realize that, even though I would never be a CEO again, I still had talents, skills and experience that other companies and individuals might benefit from. The people I caddied for, without ever knowing it, encouraged and motivated me to once again get involved in the world of entrepreneurship – the world I had known before my stroke.

## PRESS 'PLAY' AGAIN

With their encouragement, and that of my family and friends, I pushed the 'play' button again on my entrepreneurial career. As a result, over the past eight years, as well as caddying, I have been involved with many innovative and exciting businesses, whether as a director, coach or consultant. All of these businesses are 'entrepreneurial'. They are led by people who had an idea, whether it was for a product, a service or both, and then took the risk of turning it into a business. Some of these businesses are run by solo entrepreneurs, whereas others employ a lot of people. Because of this, I have I met some fascinating people who were willing to share stories, insights and ideas on many things, but especially entrepreneurship. Some of these conversations took place on the golf course when I was caddying, but others were over lunches with CEOs and entrepreneurs, at board meetings with leaders of innovative businesses, or while coaching a variety of successful (and not-so-successful) entrepreneurs.

Through my own experiences and my reflections on these conversations, I ultimately decided upon what I think is the route to success (or failure) for an entrepreneur. Success relies heavily on understanding and answering what I call the 'why' questions, as opposed to focusing on the 'how' questions.

You see, there are countless business books that ask and explain the 'how' questions: how to write a business plan; how to run a social media campaign; how to win a pitch; how to get extra investment into your business. While I acknowledge that the 'how' questions are important, I believe that asking and answering the 'why' questions leads to successful entrepreneurship. This equally applies whether you are thinking of setting up a business or whether you are currently an entrepreneur (for example, a freelancer, a solo entrepreneur, the leader of a social enterprise or the CEO of a limited company). 'Why' questions focus on topics such as why to embrace love, why you will be lonely, why it will be tough, why you need to learn how to steal, why purpose and not profit, and why you will get hurt.

When I was writing this book, sometimes these 'why' questions made me aware of the classic mistakes I made as an entrepreneurial CEO, when I thought I was doing everything right. At other times, I leaned new things about entrepreneurship, things I did not know but that are crucial for success. And finally, I am pleased to say, some of the people I talked to reinforced my existing ideas and thoughts about successful entrepreneurship. For me it is a given that, if you want success as an entrepreneur, you need passion, creativity, spontaneity and bags of energy. Sure, you need to know **how** to run a business, but it is identifying and answering for yourself the **why** questions that will lead to successful entrepreneurship.

And so, back to George. It turned out that George was a very successful undertaker who had built up a large business, employing many people. When I explained my story as I caddied for him on a lovely autumn day, he said to me, "What a great opportunity to find out not *how* people you meet became successful, but *why*." And that was the spark – the spark that led me to meet many people who helped me to discover the answers to the core 'why' questions that any entrepreneur should understand and put into action if they want sustainable success. This book that you are holding explains what these 'why' questions are and why they are important.

By beginning with a 'why' question, each chapter will focus on a core 'fundamental' required for successful and sustainable entrepreneurship, such as purpose, drive, love, desire, failure and luck. Each chapter starts with a story that highlights the 'why' question based on an experience from my life, whether from my time as a CEO, a stroke survivor, a caddie or an entrepreneur. Then the chapters explore the reason this 'why' question is important for successful entrepreneurship using practical examples, tips, simple illustrations and case studies that reinforce the message of the initial story. If you want to know more about George, you'll find him in chapter 14.

I hope you find the stories, ideas and insights in *The Entrepreneur's Book* helpful on your own entrepreneurial journey.

# 1.
# BELIEF

## THE GREAT RWANDAN
## ENTREPRENEUR

# WHY START WITH BELIEF?

A great place to start is to introduce you to one of the world's greatest living entrepreneurs – an entrepreneur whom I admire as much as Bill Gates, Richard Branson and Steve Jobs.

He is Nicholas Hitimana, CEO of Ikirezi Natural Products, an agri-business based in Rwanda. I have known Nicholas for many years, and I strongly believe that what he has achieved as an entrepreneur surpasses all of the great success stories from Silicon Valley.

You see, Nicholas, against all the odds, stuck to his belief in an idea that had the potential to bring huge positive change into the lives of large numbers of people in a country – Rwanda – where one of the world's most horrific genocides happened. This belief, a belief that he had had since he was very young, was based on a very simple principle. As he once told me on a telephone call we had together: "I **believe** that people have in themselves the potential to get out of poverty if you create the right environment that allows them to do that."

That is his core belief – and it is a belief that has driven his purpose in life and in his business. That core belief has driven him to achieve real, sustainable entrepreneurial success and fundamentally change many people's lives for the better.

Nicholas was working for a World Bank agricultural project in Rwanda when the genocide began in April 1994. In only 100 days, over 800,000 Rwandans were brutally murdered. Nicholas was able to escape with his wife and baby son and ended up in

Edinburgh in May 1995. Nicholas then successfully applied for a master's programme in Rural Development at the University of Edinburgh, which he completed in 1996. Not being able to immediately return to Rwanda, he was encouraged by the university and his friends to pursue a PhD research programme, which, again, he was successful in completing.

And here's what he did next.

In 2001, rather than getting a high-paid job in the West, Nicholas and his wife, Elsie, decided to return to Rwanda to look for new ways to create meaningful employment primarily for the widows and orphans of the genocide. With his agricultural specialization and vision, Nicholas was engaged by the Rwandan government to explore the possibility of producing essential oil from South African geranium seeds.

As a result, in 2006 Nicholas founded Ikirezi Natural Products, a community interest company, to produce high-quality essential oils in Rwanda and sell them in both Rwanda and the wider world. The profits from his company go to a series of cooperatives run by the workers to fund housing and educational projects.

Taken from an old Rwandan proverb, the word *ikirezi* means 'a precious pearl'. Nicholas views everyone who works at Ikirezi Natural Products as a unique person of innate value. Today, over 350 widows and poor farmers work at Ikirezi.

But Ikirezi is not just about employing all of these people and giving them an income. It is about Nicholas's belief that the people who work there are 'precious pearls'. Whatever these people have been through, he wants Ikirezi to create the right environment to allow them to heal and get out of poverty. More importantly, he wants Ikirezi to give them back their self-respect and their confidence so they can create a new and better future for their themselves and their families. All of this is underpinned by his belief that people have in themselves the potential to get out of poverty if you create an environment that allows them to do that.

And that is why I can say, in my humble opinion, that Nicholas is one of the world's greatest entrepreneurs. I have huge admiration for people who want to set up and run a business. However, it is one thing to set up a business, grow it successfully and employ hundreds of people in places such as the UK, Europe and the US. It takes someone with extraordinary entrepreneurial drive, talents and skills to start a business and make a success of it in a country where the idea of setting up any business would have been impossible not that long ago.

## WHAT DO YOU BELIEVE IN?

But what has this uplifting story got to do with your entrepreneurial success? Well, everything really – because defining what you believe in is the foundation that will give you your purpose as an entrepreneur. Everything is built on that!

You see, at the start of your entrepreneurial journey, your business idea is normally in your mind only, and you are the sole person who has the belief, desire and vision to envisage the great business it could become one day. You have no proof, yet, that it will work. It might be a service or a product. It might appeal to the private sector, the public sector or the voluntary sector – or all three.

But you believe in it and this belief gives you a purpose; you are driven by passion to make it happen.

Now, many of you may be thinking that having a belief in what you are doing is merely stating the obvious. But is it obvious?

If you have an idea, if you are about to set up a new business or if you are currently running a business, I want you to pause for a moment and ask yourself this question:

### Why do I want to be an entrepreneur?

My guess is that there will be range of answers, from "I think I could make a really good go at it and become very successful and wealthy" to "I've seen an opportunity in the market and I want to start a new business" to "I need to pay my mortgage and pay for my children to go to private school and I think I could earn lots of money this way" to "I just love being an entrepreneur and being my own boss, and I'm on target to be a millionaire." These answers are okay. And, if you work hard, have the right talents, build a great team around you and have a slice of luck, then you might be successful.

But are any of those answers driven by a belief in something, a purpose, or are they just a desire to be financially or materially successful?

Belief in something that gives you purpose and that you are passionate about will inspire you to achieve great things. This is the engine that drives successful entrepreneurship. Like any engine, entrepreneurship needs to cope with all types of situations.

Some of those situations will be easy, and the path you will be on will be smooth and straight. However, other situations you will find yourself in will be incredibly difficult, challenging and uncertain. Just ask Nicholas Hitimana!

So, ask yourself again: "Why do I want to be an entrepreneur?"

Here are a few possible answers:

*"I am passionate about and I believe that ... "*
*"I believe my idea will ... "*
*"I believe in this cause so much that ... "*
*"My company is based on the belief that ... "*

If you don't begin your answer with something along these lines, there is a good chance that – whether in the short, medium or long term – you will fail or give up. Crucially, you may become successful but, and it is a big 'but', deep down you will have a feeling of dissatisfaction that you just cannot put your finger on.

That is why it all starts with belief. If you don't fundamentally believe in what you are trying to achieve and why it gives you purpose, then when things get tough, you are more likely to give up. On the opposite end of the spectrum, you might achieve significant material success, but, if that success is not founded on a belief, a cause or a purpose, then deep down there will be a feeling of emptiness and a lack of meaning in what you do.

Over my years as a CEO, a caddie, a mentor and a director of several entrepreneurial companies, I have had many meetings, drunk gallons of coffee and eaten too many lunches talking to a wide range of entrepreneurs (some very successful, others less so). And I can honestly say that those who, like Nicholas, have a belief and a purpose in what they are doing are the ones who are more genuine and passionate, and who get a real sense of meaning from what they do. They believe what they are doing is important and will make a significant impact on their life and the lives of many others. Oh yes, they have bad days and weeks or even months, they have cash-flow problems and they can get incredibly stressed. Some of them have huge salaries, drive fast cars and have second homes in Europe. Others struggle to pay the mortgage, haven't been on a proper holiday for years and have a car that's eight years old. Either way, it is their belief in what they are doing that drives them on. If I ask any of them, "Why did you want to be an entrepreneur?," all their answers will have the word 'belief' in it. This is where their passion comes from and gives them their purpose as entrepreneurs.

So, don't underestimate the power of having genuine belief. If one man's belief can create a business that employs 350 widows and poor farmers in Rwanda, then it can drive you to achieve fantastic things as an entrepreneur.

# 2.
# PURPOSE

CLARITY FROM
LAKE GENEVA

# WHY PURPOSE AND NOT PROFIT?

Ali is a successful businesswoman and someone I mentor. I have known Ali for a couple years and every now and again we meet for a catch-up lunch. The last time we met, she shared with me a fascinating story about her time as a marketing manager for one of the world's global brands. You see, prior to her current job, Ali was a European marketing manager for one of the leading luxury drinks companies in the world. And it was at that point in her career that she went on a business trip to Lake Geneva that changed the direction of her life.

Ali was attending an internal company marketing conference that would last for two days. Many senior marketing people from across the world attended the conference. The agenda was packed, and there were lots of presentations and workshops.

One of these presentations was given by the marketing director of one of the company's top drinks brands, and it focused on the marketing materials that were being planned to help market this drink globally. So, during the presentation, the marketing director showed new designs for the bottle, the adverts, the website, the point-of-sale material ... and the ice buckets.

It was when the marketing director got to the part of the presentation about the ice buckets that Ali, out of nowhere, was asked for her view on the shade of blue that should be used. As Ali told me, up to that point, she had been getting more and more distracted and not really focusing on the presentation at all – her mind kept drifting to the question "Why I am here?" She managed to give a professional answer and choose one of the blues; this seemed to satisfy the marketing director, and he moved on. Finally, the session finished, and it was time for a coffee break.

At the break, Ali went and looked out of one of the five-star hotel's windows. She took in the fantastic view of Lake Geneva and thought, "What on earth am I doing talking and debating about the colours of ice buckets? Is this what I want to spend the rest of my life doing? What is the point of all of this?"

To quote Ali's words from our catch-up lunch: "I knew all about marketing. I knew *how* I did it. But I could not answer the critical 'why' question. Why was I sitting in a room in Geneva arguing about the colours of an ice bucket? And I just could not really answer that. I honestly no longer cared how much profit they would make from this new drink. Basically, even though on the surface my job gave me fantastic benefits (travel, good salary, many other benefits), it gave me no real **purpose**. I don't know how long I stood there, looking out at Lake Geneva, but in that moment, I made a conscious decision to leave my job."

Which she did! Ali had no idea what she would do, but the lack of purpose in her career drove her to leave. This search for purpose resulted in Ali spending several life-changing years working with an international charity in a senior marketing role. Her experience of working with the charity led her to the conclusion that, whereas generating profit is important to any business, purpose is fundamental.

Three years after walking away from a secure and successful job with a multinational organization, with all the trappings that it brought, Ali now works for herself as a business coach.

As she tells me, yes, she has less financial security, but she now has a purpose in what she does. When Ali coaches senior executives, she advises them that a purpose-driven organization is far more effective for everyone involved than a profit-driven organization – and she should know!

If you want to be a successful entrepreneur, you need to be purpose driven and not profit driven – regardless of what your investors might have you believe. Lead with purpose and profit will follow.

# THE PURPOSE-DRIVEN ENTREPRENEUR

I admire anyone who wants to be an entrepreneur or who is currently running a business that they started themselves. I know how incredibly difficult it is to achieve success. There will be times when you think you won't be able to pay next month's salaries. There will be times when you'll be certain that you'll make a big sale only to find out that the sale has gone to your major competitor. There will be late nights studying cash-flow forecasts, trying to figure out how you are going to survive. There will be very uncomfortable board meetings when you are challenged about the business and why it is not more successful. These are the difficult days!

On the other hand, there will be days when you pitch for new business, and it's awarded to you. There will be phone calls, out of the blue, from potential new customers who want to meet you. There will be new staff you employ who really help to drive the business forward. There will be times when you are really profitable and you have enough cash in the bank to pay the salaries for the next six months. These are the great days!

Being an entrepreneur is like riding on a rollercoaster – it has lots of ups and downs and loads of bumps. But, even though you can't level out the rollercoaster, you can put some things in place to help it be less bumpy.

So, having a belief in what you are doing as an entrepreneur will help you to have real purpose. It is this purpose that will motivate you to jump out of bed and seize the day! This purpose will shine through when you communicate about what you do and why you do it to your staff, your customers, your investors ... even to your-self. This purpose will allow you to reflect back on your day – good or bad – and say, "Yep, I know it is tough at the moment, but I also know that I am confident about my purpose, and it's not all about making money."

There is certainly good reason behind the fact that all entrepreneurs are conditioned to think that, as entrepreneurs, their number-one goal is to make a profit – no matter how long it takes. Because, regardless of what type of business you run and how much cash you have in the bank – or how much cash you might be able to access from new investors – at some point in the future, income needs to exceed expenditure. Just look at the disastrous crashes in the noughties of the dot-com businesses that ignored that rule. But chasing profits as your number-one focus can potentially lead you off course until you finally question what on earth you are doing in your life as an entrepreneur. You realize that you have no real purpose in what you do every day – a bit like what Ali experienced!

Your chances of long-term success are far greater if you lead with the pursuit of purpose, with the pursuit of profit just behind.

A purpose motivates in a way that pursuing profits alone never will – it drives you forward and gives you direction. To thrive as an entrepreneur, you need to inject your purpose into all that you do. Purpose is a key ingredient for strong, sustainable and scalable entrepreneurial success. It is an unseen-yet-ever-present element that should drive you forward as an entrepreneur.

## WHAT IS YOUR *IKIGAI*?

Nearly every week, I travel down to Newcastle because I am on the board of a software company based in that city. I enjoy the journey, not only because the scenery of the Scottish Borders and Northumberland is stunning, but also because I get the time to catch up with some of the podcasts I enjoy. One of those podcasts is *Desert Island Discs* from BBC Radio 4. The premise of *Desert Island Discs* is simple. Each week a guest, called a 'castaway' during the programme, is asked to choose eight pieces of music, a book and a luxury item that they would take if they were to be cast away on a desert island. The presenter, Kirsty Young, asks them about their choices and discusses their lives. It really is a great programme, as you find out so much about people's lives.

One of my favourite *Desert Island Discs* was the one in which Kirsty interviewed Tom Hanks, the American actor. It was a brilliant, moving and very uplifting interview. Near the end of the interview, Kirsty asked why he was still working so hard now that he was aged 60 – was it not now time to relax and enjoy life outside the movie world? But Tom essentially said that he does not see what he does as work – rather, and to use his exact words, "I am completely engaged in things that fascinate me."

That, for me, is purpose.

Let me explain further with the help of Dan Buettner, a National Geographic Fellow and *New York Times* bestselling author. In 2009, Buettner gave a TED Talk titled "How to Live to Be 100+." He talked about his work researching the world's blue zones, which are areas in which people live inordinately long, healthy lives. The blue zone with the longest disability-free life expectancy in the world is Okinawa (a Japanese island) and its surrounding archipelago. Here, people routinely live to exceed 100 years of age. At this age, they are still physically capable, fully alert and involved in the world around them. They work in their gardens and play with their great-grandchildren, and when they die it generally happens quickly and in their sleep. Their rates of disease are many times lower than those in much of the rest of the world.

Interestingly, Okinawans don't have a word for retirement. What they have is *ikigai*, which roughly translated means 'passion' or 'reason for living'. When he conducted his study with the Okinawans, one of the questions in Buettner's questionnaire was, "What is your *ikigai*?" Nearly all of the people were able to answer immediately. For a 102-year-old karate master, his *ikigai* was to teach his martial art. For a 100-year-old fisherman, it was going out and bringing fish back to his family three days each week. For a 102-year-old woman, her *ikigai* was to spend time with her great-great-granddaughter. These were their 'reasons for living' – their purpose.

To be a successful entrepreneur, you need to find out what your *ikigai* is. Purpose is not a static thing – throughout their lives, the Okinawans interviewed by Buettner had identified the purpose of why they did the things they did.

Identifying what your purpose is as an entrepreneur can be diffi-cult, but it is crucial. If you struggle to identify what your current purpose is, then a good starting point is to try to answer these four simple but thought-provoking questions:

1. **What do you love?** The answer to this is your passion.
2. **What are you good at?** The answer to this is your mission.
3. **What can you be paid for?** The answer to this is your profession.
4. **What does the world need?** The answer to this is your vocation.

If you can answer those four questions, then you have probably identified your current purpose (*ikigai*) as an entrepreneur, and that is crucial achievement.

Going back to Ali, she certainly did not find her *ikigai* when she worked for the global drinks company. But she did a very brave thing – when she realized that she could see no purpose in what she did in her current role, she came to the conclusion that it was time to move on. Understanding why it is so important to have an identifiable purpose in what you do, being able to communicate it, and living and breathing it every day will increase your chances of long-term success as an entrepreneur tenfold.

# 3.
# VALUES

## THE 'HAAR'

# WHY KNOW YOUR VALUES?

I must say, I am very fortunate to live in a place like North Berwick, Scotland. It is a beautiful, scenic and friendly place to live. It has some great bars, cafés, shops and restaurants, as well as some stunning beaches.

One stunning August day, I was walking my two dogs on the beach when a family cycled past and I heard the mother say to her two children, "What an idyllic place." The tide was out, the sun was shining, there wasn't a cloud in the sky and there was only a gentle breeze.

It was a day not dissimilar to that one on the beach when I caddied for Ben, who was from San Diego, California. Ben was with seven other friends, and it turned out that this was an annual trip to come and play golf in Scotland.

As we walked onto the first green, rather than going to line up his putt, Ben went over to his golf bag and took out his camera. He then proceeded to take at least ten pictures, and when he had finished he turned to me and said, "Man, this place is fantastic – it looks and feels like parts of California!" Even though I have never been to California, I understood what he meant – it really was a lovely, still day.

Ben was a good golfer, and as we went around the course he told me that he was one of the founders of a very successful computer gaming company based in California. When he told me that, I turned to him and said, laughing, "At last."

"At last what?" he replied.

"At last I can come home from caddying and impress my youngest son about caddying for someone 'cool'!"

Ben laughed and told me about some of the games he promotes and markets. Even I knew what they were. My son was going to be very impressed!

We then chatted about his job further – specifically about how competitive and difficult it was to design and then market a new game successfully.

"So," I asked, "on average, how much is it to design, build and then market a successful game?"

Ben told me that there is no specific number because all games are slightly different. However, it can take years to develop and build a game, so we were talking millions of dollars. I was staggered, and he could see it in my face. How little did I know!

"It's a risky business, but we've been doing it for a while so we know what we're doing. So far, in the main, it has been very successful," he said with a smile.

As Ben was happy to chat about his work, I explained to him about my role as a consultant helping entrepreneurial digital companies to grow and expand. He seemed genuinely intrigued that his caddie was also a digital consultant. So we chatted a bit more and the conversation led me to ask him what he thought was the most important thing – the number-one factor – to build a successful company.

He thought for a while and then said this: "For me, the number-one thing is to define what your values are as a business and build your business on those values – everything comes from that." I must say, I thought that was great. Normally, when I ask people that question, they say things like 'passion' or 'creativity' or 'hard work', but never 'values'.

We continued to chat, and then as we walked along the 14th fairway something started to happen that usually means the end of the golf round. It wasn't strong winds and pouring rain – you can play through those. No, it was what we call in Scotland the 'haar' (fog), which had started to come in from the sea. Standing on the 14th green, I turned to Ben and pointed towards a blanket of haar that was quickly moving towards us and said, "This isn't good – but hopefully it won't last."

"Yep," he said, "just like California. Well, San Francisco to be specific!"

Then suddenly the beautiful, clear day was no longer. The haar engulfed the whole golf course, and we couldn't see further than 50 feet. Normally, during these conditions the game stops and you walk back to the clubhouse.

Instead, Ben, the rest of the group and I waited on the 14th green to see what would happen – would the haar lift or would the siren sound, meaning we needed to leave the golf course? We stood on the green for about ten minutes and then fortunately the haar started to lift. We could suddenly see into the distance. Then, as quickly as the haar had descended on us, it went and the beautiful day returned.

As we walked off the 14th green, Ben said something fascinating: "There you go," he said, "a perfect analogy for building a successful business. Having a set of values for your business and sticking with them is similar to what has just happened. For 14 holes we knew where we were going, but suddenly the haar appeared and for a while we could hardly see anything. Nevertheless, we waited and waited and eventually the haar did lift. So, sticking to your values, even when things get tough (like when the haar engulfs you) for a while, is one of the most important things you can do in business."

That, to me, is one of the best business analogies I have ever heard.

## ENTREPRENEURIAL VALUES

Ben was talking about values – the principles that you stick with. These are the values around which any entrepreneur should base all their decisions, plan strategies and interact with staff, customers, suppliers and investors.

So, today, whatever stage you are at as an entrepreneur, what are your values? What are the values that are important to you? What are the things that would lead you to say 'no' to a great opportunity because it did not tally with these values? Your values are the things that you believe are important in the way you live and work. Your values should determine your priorities, what you will spend your time on and how you will engage with people. Everything you do and the way you behave and act should match your values as an entrepreneur – when that is the case, life generally feels better and you are more contented even though there will always be difficult days or weeks or even years.

However, if you don't really know what your values are or what you 'stand for', then the chances are that you will be stuck in the haar, unable to visualize what is ahead of you, constantly stumbling from one project or business to another, perhaps giving up when things get difficult, doing things that give you short-term success but that you end up regretting in the long term. This is why it is so important for every entrepreneur to make a conscious effort to identify their values.

So, whether you are a one-person, a start-up or an established business, your values should always align with your beliefs and your purpose, whatever you do as an entrepreneur. In general, your values should be the values that you want to base all aspects of your life on – not only your entrepreneurial life. This means you will be true to yourself in everything you do. The values that you run your business on should be no different from the values you demonstrate to your family and friends.

Having defined values is like writing an autobiography or making a brilliant film about your own life in reverse – you start with the ending! Imagine you're writing the last few sentences in your autobiography, closing with the words, "Finally, throughout my career as an entrepreneur, I have stuck to these values and have always believed in them." What would those values be? Those values should be constant and should not really change throughout your entrepreneurial life. They are what will drive you and keep you on the right path – no matter how tough things become, they will inspire you. Values are guiding principles that determine how you will act as an entrepreneur – they will shine a light on everything you do as an entrepreneur to keep you true to yourself.

# TURING FEST

Over the past few years, a tech festival conference has been taking place in Edinburgh: Turing Fest. I attended the year I was writing this book, and it was a brilliant event. Most of the presenters are experts in their field, and a number of the presentations are given by founders, CEOs or senior people of successful digital businesses.

One of the presentations was given by a senior person from the digital company Buffer. Buffer's product allows individuals and companies to schedule and share their social media content via social media sites such as Facebook, LinkedIn and Twitter at the best possible times that suit them throughout the day.

Buffer is a fascinating business. It has no office and no fixed or minimum hours for its staff. The Buffer team works from multiple countries and continents. They believe that living in a place that makes them happy is crucial to making Buffer successful. The company currently employs around 75 people from around the world. They use a variety of technical tools that help them to communicate and collaborate with each other. Through these tools, they aim to share everything about the business with their employees – financial reports, marketing plans and even salaries!

The CEO and the senior team believe that this philosophy makes the company incredibly productive, because people are living and working in an environment that makes them happy and content – whether that's their home, the local coffee shop or a hot-desk office set-up.

And do you know what is at the core of what allows Buffer to do this? There are ten values that the people at Buffer believe in and stick to. These values drive every decision they make. The ten values are:

**CHOOSE POSITIVITY**
DEFAULT TO TRANSPARENCY
**FOCUS ON SELF-IMPROVEMENT**
BE A NO-EGO DOER
**LISTEN FIRST, THEN LISTEN MORE**
COMMUNICATE WITH CLARITY
**MAKE TIME TO REFLECT**
LIVE SMARTER, NOT HARDER
**SHOW GRATITUDE**
DO THE RIGHT THING

As the Buffer representative said in her presentation, "These values of Buffer decide if, how and why we do anything." Basically, whatever they do as a business, if it doesn't align with these values, they just don't do it.

Now, I have no idea how successful or not Buffer will be in the long term, but what I do know, from sitting and listening to this presentation, is that the company has a great chance. Its employees genuinely seem to be driven by their values. I would love to work for Buffer, as their business values align with some of mine and none conflict – although having looked at their profiles and pictures, I fear that I may be a little too old!

So, like Buffer did, write down your own entrepreneurial values and refer to them constantly until they are 'tattooed' onto your brain. Any time you need to make a big decision, always refer back to them. If you feel your values could or will be comprised, then don't do the thing you're considering. If, however, it aligns with your values and there is no conflict, then go for it and you will not be stuck in the haar – on the contrary, it will be a clear and beautiful day.

# 4.
# DESIRE

BE LIKE BERNIE

# WHY DO YOU NEED TO OVERCOME FEAR?

Sometimes you meet people for the first time and you instantly say to yourself, "I think I'm really going to like you." That is exactly how I felt when I first met Bernie, on the beach at North Berwick, when I was out walking my dogs.

You see, our oldest dog, Dougal, has perfected the art of what we call 'working the beach'. He trots up to anyone he thinks will be interested in him with the sole intention of seeing whether they have food in their pocket. He does this brilliantly, I have to say. He chooses his potential target carefully. Top of the list will be someone who has a dog themselves, especially if they have children with them. And the bigger the group the better, as far as Dougal is concerned. Once he has a target, he wanders up to them, tail wagging, body getting lower to the ground, until he is nearly crawling. Then he will either fall on his side or sit on their feet. His strategy nearly always works. Nine times out of ten, the target looks at me and asks, "Is it okay if I give him a wee treat?" and I always say yes. Dougal then eats the treat, wags his tail and wanders off to find his next target.

And that is how I got to meet Bernie for the first time. Bernie was out walking with her spaniel and her two children when Dougal spotted her. Off he went, employing his normal technique, and as ever it worked perfectly.

"Hi, what a great dog," Bernie said. "I think he can smell the dog treat in my pocket – would it be okay if I gave him one?"

I said yes and then I turned to Dougal and said, "Worked again, Dougal."

Bernie laughed and we got chatting. It turned out that she had moved from the west coast of Scotland to North Berwick with her family in 2005. She had given up her role as a sales director for a commercial wall-covering company when her kids came along. A few years later they made the decision, as a family, to live by the beach, as Bernie had always had the dream from a young age to do that. Just from that initial chat, I could feel she was a warm, genuine and friendly person, and I instantly liked her.

That was seven years ago, and since then we have become good friends. I admire Bernie and can't help but find her inspirational. She took the risk of ripping up the rule book by following her intuition to live by the beach in order to do something different, even though she had no idea at the time what that was going to be. One day, when we chatted about that decision, she said, "I just had a gut feeling that I needed to do something else, even though I didn't know what that would be."

But that gut feeling was crystallized into a business idea in 2011 when Bernie was out running on the beach. Bernie's interest in yoga, meditation and holistic therapies had been awakened in her the previous year. That morning as she ran, an idea started to form in her mind – why not set up a wellbeing business in North Berwick that combined coaching and workshops with her love for yoga, meditation and holistic therapies? By the end of the run, Bernie had decided she had finally found something she really wanted to do with her life. She wanted to create a space where people could do things like dance, yoga or meditation, or whatever form of holistic exercise floated their boat. It would be a place where people could experience these things in a safe and welcoming environment that would help them reconnect with themselves.

The idea became a reality when she signed a lease in 2014 for a building in North Berwick that is now called the Barefoot Sanctuary. It has a studio that is used for many things, including yoga, company retreats and exercise classes. It has rooms for one-to-one coaching and mentoring. It is used seven days a week and has brought many positive benefits to the people of North Berwick and beyond.

To me, Bernie is a wonderful entrepreneur. I really admire what she has achieved, and I wanted to share her story with you. One day, when I asked her what drove her to go for it and set up the Barefoot Sanctuary, she said, "The **desire** of actually going for it and committing to do it outweighed the fear of not doing it."

This is what drove Bernie to take an idea and turn it into a reality. She did not want to live with the regrets of not having made a go of her idea. She never let go of her belief that she could make the Barefoot Sanctuary a reality and a success. The desire outweighed the fear of not doing it. This resulted in a great business that benefits not only Bernie and her family, but also the people of North Berwick and beyond who use the Barefoot Sanctuary.

My guess is that Bernie had all the fears that people have when they want to do something new with their lives. She would have had fears around many things, such as how to pay the mortgage if things didn't go to plan, what would happen if no one booked classes at the Barefoot Sanctuary or what people would think of her if the business failed. But her desire to do something differ-ent, to make her dream become a reality, was strong and helped her overcome her fears. Now her life is more fulfilling, rewarding and satisfying than it has ever been.

So, I must thank Dougal for 'introducing' me to Bernie, as she demonstrates that one of the critical ingredients for successful entrepreneurship is a desire to go for it, regardless of how scared you are of failure.

# WE HAVE ALWAYS DONE IT THIS WAY
To me, desire is a crucial factor for successful entrepreneurship. The desire to do something must outweigh the fear of not doing it.

There are so many people who have dreams, ideas and plans – who want to set up a business, or become an author, a musician or an artist, or work in another country – but their fear of potential failure outweighs their desire to actually do these things. Therefore, fear wins, and they don't do what their gut or intuition is telling them do. And in the medium to long term, they probably regret it.

There are many entrepreneurs running start-ups or established businesses who still let the fear beat the desire to do something innovative, new or different that could potentially take them to the next stage of success. And so, the business bumbles along, per-haps with cash-flow issues and struggling sales performance. They fear that if they change sales strategy or if they increase their over-draft to invest in new technology or a second office, they might fail. Even though the rational part of their thinking and their intuition are telling them to go for it, they don't. They procrastinate, they stall, they kid, they make excuses because of fear. The fear wins and the desire to do something better is put on hold yet again.

But part of successful entrepreneurship is overcoming fear. It is about taking risks every day. It is about challenging your own thinking and not allowing yourself to rest on your laurels. It is about managing the fear that is telling you not to do something when you know, in your heart, that you need to go for it. This can apply to the small things, such as making that cold call to a potential new client you just read an article about in a newspaper, and to the big things, such as re-mortgaging your house to make a new major investment in your business to help it grow and expand.

Now, not for one moment am I suggesting you make rash decisions or decisions that you have not thought through with others whom you trust and admire. That would be foolish and unwise. But there is a danger that entrepreneurs will fall into a trap based on fear, believing that nothing needs to change and everything is okay. They start to believe in the statement 'we have always done it this way' and question why they should try something new. But for me that statement is one of the most dangerous traps for an entrepreneur, as it is built on fear, not desire. At best that philosophy will hold you back, and at worst it will ultimately lead to failure. Maybe not now, but sometime down the line. Okay, the business might survive, but the passion, the excitement and the buzz will have long gone. Businesses like this might grow for a while. They might have short-term success. But in the long term they will fail. Fear of change, fear of innovation and fear to challenge the norm will win. Yes, the business might stagger along, but the entrepreneur, who once had all those dreams of success, will not see it as a success.

So, be like Bernie and don't let fear extinguish the desire to do something different, something that you know is the right thing to do.

# THE TUSCANY RISK

Now would be a good point to share with you a very personal story about my parents, who showed me the benefits of allowing desire to overcome fear.

My parents were both born in the northeast of England – my dad in Durham, my mum in a small village close to Sunderland. They got married in 1949 and then in the fifties they had my sister and my brother. At that point in their lives, my dad had a job at a clothing company, where he made suits, and my mum brought up the family. My mum had never travelled out of the northeast of England and my dad had only left the area once, and that had been when he served in the army in 1946–1947.

But, at the end of the fifties, 1959 to be precise, when my sister was eight and my brother was five, my parents made the brave decision to move the family to Italy. Today, moving to Tuscany and living there sounds fantastic – all that great food, wine and scenery. But this was 60 years ago, when my parents could not speak a word of Italian, had never ventured any farther than the northeast of England and had no idea what life would be like for them in Italy. So why did they go? Well, my dad proudly shared their story with me many a time.

Back in 1959, they were not living in a nice area and the prospect of bringing up two children where they were was not too attractive.

Yes, Dad had a job, but it was not rewarding and the prospects were limited. So, one evening he came home from work, sat at the kitchen table and said to Mum, "Life must have more to offer than this." From that point on, the desire to do something different formed in their minds, although neither of them were at all clear about what it would be.

A few weeks later, Dad was having his lunch at work. One of his colleagues knew that he wanted to try something new and had seen a job advert in the local newspaper. He cut the advert out of the paper and gave it to my dad at lunchtime. The job advert was looking for a 'cutting manager' (someone who could manage a team of suit makers) to be based in Carrara, Tuscany. Dad took the advert home that evening, talked to Mum and then decided to apply for the position. I don't think he ever expected to get the job (his manager was also applying!) but, he was determined to go for it nonetheless and to try something new. And do you know what – against all the odds, my dad was offered the role. Two months later, my mum, dad, brother and sister were waved off from Durham railway station by their extended families.

Ultimately, my parents lived in Carrara for a total of six years. Initially it was very difficult. But, once they had learned some Italian and begun to understand Italian culture, they absolutely loved it. They experienced a new world: they travelled across Italy for holidays, made some fabulous friends, ate wonderful food and drank lovely wine. Yes, they worked very hard, but they also experienced things that they had never even dreamed of. So, you might ask, why did they come back? Well, blame me (my sister and brother still do!). Mum became pregnant in 1964, and they decided that it would be a good time to move back to England from Italy.

So Dad was transferred to another part of the business just outside Manchester, and that is where we all lived.

This very personal story about my parents shows perfectly the power of allowing your desire to do something new, innovative or challenging overcome the fear of not doing it. If my parents had allowed fear to win and not gone to Italy, there's every chance their lives would not have been so fulfilling and exciting as they turned out to be. My sister and brother would not have had the same opportunities that were presented to them in Italy. And, crucially for me, I may not have been born!

# 5.
# LOVE

## KNOW THE
## CLEANER'S NAME

# WHY ACT WITH LOVE?

Over the past eight years, I have been involved with a number of digital and software start-up companies as a consultant, mentor or board member, and I really enjoy doing it. Most of them realize that they don't have the experience of running a business, and they are keen to seek help and advice. That is where I come in. In the main, I am used as a sounding board for new ideas, I provide support and guidance to the leadership team, and I attend regular board meetings.

The board meetings tend to have very similar agenda formats – finance, sales and marketing, product update, HR and any other business. Sounds boring! Well, sometimes it seems like Groundhog Day, as one meeting feels just like the one before, until you get to the last agenda item – any other business. You really have no idea what will come up here. These are the agenda items that do not fit into any other agenda sections, and I tend to hold my breath as I wait to hear what bombshell might be dropped on the business. For example, the CEO might decide that they deserve a sabbatical or the sales director might think we should open an office abroad even with poor sales. However, sometimes something comes up that really shows the true nature of the leadership team.

The following story shows the true nature of an excellent leadership team and demonstrates one of the most important principles any entrepreneur should have – **love**.

This is a great company to be involved with. For confidentiality reasons, and you will see why as I tell their story, I will not be naming the company, and I will be using pseudonyms. The team are full of energy and passion and are driven by a belief, a purpose and a set of values that I am sure will make them very successful. Crucially, they are led by a CEO, Luke, who inspires the whole team.

Recently I was asked to chair a board meeting because the customary chair was on holiday. The board meeting was a good one – not at all because of my chairing skills, but because the financial results were good and the sales and marketing activity were very positive. Before finishing the meeting, I went around the table (there were six people at the meeting) and asked if there was any other business. Everyone said no until I asked Luke.

"Well," he said, "there is one thing and I didn't know whether I should bring it up, but I feel I am out of my depth."

"Okay, what is it?" I replied.

"So," Luke said, "you know Martha, one of our digital designers? Well, in the past, she has had bouts of depression. I was aware of it when I employed her, and over the past year I have been paying for private psychological support for her. She has been a great employee, but now and again she is so depressed that she cannot face coming into work. And I have been fine with that as the work she does when she is here is excellent."

I had been unaware of this, but it didn't surprise me that Luke had offered to fund Martha's support – supporting people is just one of the values he believes in.

He continued: "About two weeks ago, things took a turn for the worse – she overdosed on painkillers on a Sunday evening. Fortunately, one of her flatmates found her, unconscious, and called an ambulance. Martha doesn't have any family members living close by, so her flatmate called me and I rushed to the hospital, and I stayed with her that evening until she was conscious and was transferred to a ward. I then spent three days going back and forth to the hospital visiting her. I had to cancel all my appointments for those three days – one of which was a big pitch for some new business. She is now back at home, and I have popped in to see her every day since, but I don't know when she will get back to work. I feel that I am out of my depth now. I think it is really important that we support Martha, whatever happens, but I don't know whether we should recruit a new designer or wait until she comes back."

We discussed the options that were open to us and agreed what we would do in supporting Martha going forward. Luke had surprised us all and I felt I had to let him know that he had done far more than most CEOs that I know and give him credit for taking on the responsibility of caring for Martha.

Luke was reassured and told me how he strongly believes in valuing employees at work, and in their private lives, and that it is something he would hope others would do for him if he were in a similar situation.

Luke saw Martha not only as an important member of the team, but also as a human being who needed support and love through a very difficult time of her life. Luke saw his role as CEO as covering a much wider remit than just running the business;

he felt his role encompassed caring and valuing all of his staff, both at work and personally, and that is why I think Luke is a great entrepreneur – he 'walks the talk' in valuing his staff. Basically, Luke was demonstrating love!

## LOVABLE ENTREPRENEURSHIP

Now, 'love' is a word we don't normally associate with entrepreneurship, apart from through the old adage 'love what you do'. What I am talking about here and what Luke demonstrated is love based on warmth, affection, valuing and connection to all those around us. This applies whether you are a solo entrepreneur or running a large business. When I mention love in this context, think compassion, not passion! We're talking caring, bonding, small kindnesses and concern for others over our own needs.

Why is it so important for an entrepreneur to demonstrate love, you might ask? Because the outcomes of doing it will make your entrepreneurial journey so much more enjoyable and successful. If people who work for you genuinely believe that you love them, then they will feel more valued and will go that extra mile for you. When you ask employees to work over the weekend, for no pay, because cash flow is tight and you have a client that needs a job delivered by Monday morning, then they are more likely to do it if they feel they are valued.

If you support and love your staff, or your suppliers or your customers, during the difficult times then they will be more loyal.

As Clarence Francis, Chairman of General Foods in the 1940s, acknowledged:

*You can buy a man's life, you can buy a man's physical presence at a given place; you can even buy a measured number of skilled muscular motions per hour or day. But you cannot buy enthusiasm; you cannot buy initiative; you cannot buy loyalty; you cannot buy the devotion of hearts, minds and souls. You have to earn these things.*

As an entrepreneur, if you only emphasize your skill, capability and talents to all around you then, unfortunately, I think that is the wrong approach. Why? Well, it's simple really. When the people you work with decide whom to respect, trust and follow, they will not, in the long term, judge you entirely based on how strong you are (your skill, capability or competence). Rather, they will also 'look' at how lovable you are – do they see someone they trust, who is warm and gives them a sense of value about who they are as an individual? If they do, then your chances of real, sustainable success as an entrepreneur will increase significantly.

Martha, I know, really appreciated the care and love that Luke showed her. My guess is that most people would prefer to feel they are valued and loved rather than getting a small pay rise!

# Q12

Every month, I have coffee and a catch-up with a very good friend, Gavin. Gavin is passionate about the benefits that entrepreneurs and others derive from giving 'experiences of being valued'. For him, the evidence is clear: levels of customer satisfaction, profitability, productivity and employee engagement are all enhanced when 'experiencing being valued' becomes the culture in your relationships with your team, your customers and your suppliers.

Gavin is the co-founder of a consultancy, Value the Person International, that promotes this belief.

Over coffee, while I couldn't name any names, I gave Gavin the gist of what Luke had done for Martha. He went on to tell me how his beliefs about experiences of being valued had been affirmed by one of the world's largest research projects into employee engagement, run by Gallup.

As of this writing, Gallup's most recent report on this subject is titled *State of the American Workplace*. Gallup interviewed hundreds of thousands of workers in the US over a three-year period about how they feel about their jobs. The key finding was that only 30% of these employees were fully engaged in their jobs – in other words, less than a third loved what they did and felt valued! The rest either *felt* disengaged or actively *were* disengaged from their jobs.

This research is based on what Gallup calls the Gallup Q12. These questions measure the climate of a workplace, employees' perceptions of what they get in terms of direction and resources, what they can give in terms of using their strengths and how they are valued, whether they have a sense of belonging and whether they are growing.

These are the 12 questions:

1. Do I know what is expected of me at work?
2. Do I have the materials and equipment I need to do my work right?
3. At work, do I have the opportunity to do what I do best every day?

4. In the last seven days, have I received recognition or praise for doing good work?
5. Does my supervisor, or someone at work, seem to care about me as a person?
6. Is there someone at work who encourages my development?
7. At work, do my opinions seem to count?
8. Does the mission/purpose of my company make me feel my job is important?
9. Are my co-workers committed to doing quality work?
10. Do I have a best friend at work?
11. In the last six months, has someone at work talked to me about my progress?
12. This last year, have I had opportunities at work to learn and grow?

I was fascinated by all of this. Gavin explained that all the evidence shows that those companies – small or large – that score very highly on the Gallup Q12 will do better, in all areas, as companies and that the people who work there will feel valued and loved, and will enjoy their jobs.

As we continued our discussion, I strongly felt the need for an additional 13th question that would apply only to CEOs and people in leadership positions:

13. What is the name of the person who cleans your office?

There is no empirical evidence that knowing the name of your cleaner will make you a better entrepreneur, but my intuition tells me it will. You see, I think that, as an entrepreneur, if you really want success, then you need to create an environment in which the people who work for you, and the clients you work for, sense a feeling of value and love oozing out of you. Knowing the name of your cleaner, and a bit about their life, shows in a small way that you value everyone who works with you. For me, the best entrepreneurs are those who can inspire, not only through their belief, purpose and values, but also through their kindness, flexibility, support and empowerment. When you treat people with love they never forget and, as a result, you develop people who want to work with you because you care. In this way, strong bonds are formed and trust is established, and you will be seen as an entrepreneur people really love.

Don't underestimate the power of that!

# 6.
# MORALS

TWO STORIES

# WHY DO YOU NEED A LINE?

You have probably noticed that over the past couple of decades there have been several TV programmes focusing on entrepreneurship. One of the most successful of these is *The Apprentice*. The premise of the show is that a group of aspiring businesspeople compete against each other in a series of business-related challenges in order to win a £250,000 investment in their own business offered by the British business magnate Lord Alan Sugar. Each week the contestants are split into two teams and asked to compete in a challenge. The losing team must then appear in Lord Sugar's boardroom to explain why they lost. At the end of this interview, Lord Sugar decides which individual(s) on the losing team will be 'fired' and leave the show. In the final episode, there are only two contestants left and one is 'hired', securing the £250,000 investment and becoming Lord Sugar's business partner.

I must admit I do enjoy the show – it has a great mixture of 'interesting' contestants, to say the least. It also uses some excellent business challenges and demonstrates, in some ways, what is required to be a successful entrepreneur. However, there is one aspect of the show that makes me uncomfortable. It seems to advocate that, for some contestants, anything is acceptable to try and win; at times it even seems like bending the truth – or actually deceiving – is deemed to be okay. For me, this presents a problem, as it shows a bad side of entrepreneurship.

The flip side of this win-at-any-cost attitude is shown in the following story.

In around 2005, I asked a very successful entrepreneur, Paul, to mentor me in my CEO role and be my sounding board. Paul had made millions in growing and selling a number of businesses and was well known in business circles. He was keen to help me, and every couple of months we would meet for dinner to bounce around ideas and for me to get his thoughts on everything from staff issues to strategies for attracting new clients. It was at one of those dinners that we had a conversation that I remember very well, since it had an incredibly profound impact on me.

That evening, we had been talking about business development and how difficult I was finding it to attract new clients. During that part of the conversation, Paul said, "I want to ask you two very important questions. Firstly, is there anything you would not do to secure a contract with a new client and, secondly, would you work with any type of client?"

I thought about this for a while before replying that yes, I would do anything to win new work as my business employed many people and we had significant overheads. I felt that securing a deal was the most important thing for any entrepreneur.

To my surprise, Paul disagreed with me and explained that there were certain business sectors that he would not work with. For example, from day one of starting his first business, he decided that he would not work for any clients in the defence industry. He said, "In my heart, I am a pacifist and for me it would be very hypocritical to have clients in that sector. Over the years, I have turned down significant contracts with companies that were associated with the defence industry."

Paul explained that there needs to be a line that is not crossed, regardless of how tempting it may appear to be to do so. Business is not just about making money at any cost – having a **moral** and ethical line that is never crossed can help entrepreneurs find real meaning in their work.

So, there you have two stories: one that shows anything is acceptable in business as long as you win and you get the deal, and one where a line is in play that will never be crossed.

Now, I am not advocating which path you should choose. But, 12 years on from that conversation, I think Paul was correct. As an entrepreneur, having a line that you will not cross – a moral and ethical code – is a key component towards giving you a real sense of meaning in what you do. And, at the end of the day, is that not what every entrepreneur strives for – meaning, not just huge salaries or expensive cars?

So, how can having a line help give you meaning in what you do as an entrepreneur?

## YOUR MORAL CODE

As you are probably aware, one of the brilliant benefits of being an entrepreneur is that you can set the rules. Those rules cover everything from the culture you foster in your business to the hours you work, the people you employ and the clients you work with. Crucially, you also get the opportunity to set the lines that you will not cross. And, trust me, having those lines is important. It might be that, like Paul, there are certain sectors that you won't work with because of a certain moral view. Whatever your lines are, they can give you meaning in your quest for success and a sense of value and pride in what you do – a real sense of meaning in what you are trying to achieve.

However, it is no surprise that entrepreneurs struggle to stick to their principles and values, because business, principles and values can make very uncomfortable bedfellows. For example, to my knowledge none of the MBA courses in the top three UK universities have modules on morals or ethics. And, for me, it comes as no surprise when we hear about greedy bankers, offshore accounts and tax-avoidance schemes.

Alternatively, just switch on the TV or go to the cinema. Not only do TV programmes promote an 'anything is acceptable' culture in business, but Hollywood has its fair share of the 'greed is good' philosophy. Think *Wall Street, Glengarry Glen Ross, The Wolf of Wall Street* and *The Big Short*, to name a few.

And I get that totally! Because in the early years of my entrepreneurial life, winning the deal was my number-one objective. At times, to achieve that, I did compromise my personal values or ignore my principles in order to grow my business – and I regret that. I have found that the short-term quick fix of winning at any cost and the buzz you get from that have had later consequences for me, my business, my staff and my clients. And the biggest consequence of it all is the loss of respect and trust of your staff, clients and suppliers.

The best compliment you can receive as an entrepreneur is not that you did a great job or that you are innovative or that people really like you (though they are all important!), but that people trust you: they see that you have integrity, are authentic and are consistent. Earning the trust and respect of clients, suppliers and employees is a hugely important aspect of being an entrepreneur.

And in part this comes from setting a line in terms of your values and principles that you will not compromise. With that line comes a benchmark for what you will and will not do in business. Sticking to your line can give you a strong feeling of meaning in what you do as an entrepreneur.

# 7.
# OWNERSHIP

## THE SEATTLE
## FISHMONGERS

# WHY IS IT ALL 'OVER HERE'?

I have caddied for hundreds of people, worked with many entrepreneurs and met many successful business leaders. And I have come to this conclusion: the little insights and ideas that they share with me about entrepreneurship tend to be more powerful and thought-provoking than their long stories and complex anecdotes. What is great is that these insights and thoughts come from a wide range of people – the leaders of some of the biggest companies in the world, but also dentists, truck drivers, technology specialists, teachers, entrepreneurs and personal assistants, to name a few.

All I need to do to access this world of wisdom is to listen to what people share with me or what they chat about with their friends. What is brilliant is that most of the time they don't realize how wise they are or how perceptive they are being – they are just saying it as they see it. A great example of this is when I caddied for Tom from Michigan.

After the introductions on the first tee, Tom asked me to take a photo of his group. All eight of them were so full of excitement and laughing and joking so much that it took about five minutes to take the photo. As we walked up the first fairway, I began chatting to Tom.

"I have to say, you seem to be just a little bit happy to be here!" I said.

"Absolutely," replied Tom. "It's just brilliant to be here at last – we have been planning this trip for about three years. So, take me around your golf course – you give me the yardage and the line and I'll hit the shots."

Tom's enthusiasm for playing golf was great, and I knew it was going to be a good round. It turned out that Tom and the seven other people in his group had all been at college together and had known each other for at least 20 years. They all had different careers, with Tom being the owner of a training company that ran sales coaching and courses for some of the US's biggest companies. As well as his infectious enthusiasm, Tom had a warm and welcoming personality. He was keen for me to give him advice on which shots to use, and he was also fascinated about the history of the course and the landmarks he could see as we played our round.

And then something happened: on the seventh hole, one of those little insights I mentioned earlier sparked a train of thought in my head.

Let me explain. The seventh is a great but very difficult hole. It is not long, about 340 yards, but the green is protected by a big 'burn' (stream). Everyone drives short of the burn and then the second shot needs to be perfect – too short and you will end up in the burn; too long and you will land either in one of the bunkers or in the rough that surrounds the green at the sides and at the back. The green is massive and it is not flat – there are lots of burrows to overcome. The pitfalls are many! So, if your shot to the green is not perfect, you will find yourself in the burn or a bunker, or facing a huge putt or the rough. And the last of these was exactly what happened to Tom.

He hit a good drive that left him with about 100 yards to the flag. He asked me which club he should hit and I suggested a pitching wedge, which he agreed with. He then hit the shot. As soon as he did, I knew the distance was a bit long and that the direction was a bit off. The ball cleared the burn and then the green and landed in the rough! Tom now had a very difficult third shot.

I told Tom that I felt bad about landing him a tricky shot now and that I should have recommended a different club. But he reassured me that it was okay, because it had been his decision in the end. "I played the shot, not you," he said.

It took Tom another five shots to finish the hole – a seven on a par-four hole. As we walked towards the eighth hole, I told him that his attitude was refreshing, as a lot of golfers try to blame the caddie for a poor shot.

He turned and said, "It is all about **ownership**, Neil. Why would I blame you? I chose to use that pitching wedge, I hit the shot, I missed the putts – not you. I have always had the philosophy that you should never blame people for your own decisions. It has served me well both in business and in golf – you are responsible for your decisions, nobody else."

Now that, for me, is one of those brilliant little insights that I have been talking about.

These insights, which seem so simple, straightforward and obvious when you hear them first, can suddenly seem universally applicable to all areas of your life, including entrepreneurship. As I thought more about this, I realized Tom was a perfect illustration of the importance of ownership – owning your actions and being responsible for everything you do. As an entrepreneur, everything you do – small or big – starts and finishes with you. If you foster the idea of ownership, then you will be on the right path to success. But, if you try to pass the buck or blame others for your own bad decisions or failures, then you will be on the path to failure.

I now believe that ownership is one of the most crucial and fundamental parts of being an entrepreneur – and it all came from a little insight from Tom from Michigan.

## DON'T BLAME

The easiest thing to do when things are not going well for you as an entrepreneur is to blame other people: clients, suppliers, the bank, accountants, lawyers, funders or fate. Whatever it is, there is always someone else to blame. Blame is a great tool to make you feel better temporarily. It can, for a short time, take the pressure off you. However, in the longer term, it will backfire on you.

Trust me, I used blame many times when I was a CEO rather than accepting, and owning, the bad decisions I made. I can look back and remember blaming my sales manager for a contract we should have won but lost to our main competitor. But who had signed off the proposal document and led the pitch? Me! On another occasion, I was furious with my HR manager about an employee who had a terrible attendance record, and I blamed her for the problems that employee was causing us. But who had been in the final interview when we gave the employee a job? Me!

Because the decisions I had made had not turned out well, I needed someone to blame. And that kind of blame can destroy team spirit and foster a culture characterized by an unwillingness on the part of staff to take risks or accept responsibility for mistakes due to fear of criticism or repercussions. In hindsight, I now know that I should have owned all of those decisions and lived with the consequences. At the end of the day, they were my decisions and no one else's.

## PIKE PLACE FISH

Years ago, a close friend gave me a great book that illustrates the power of ownership. In the book is a brilliant little statement that defines ownership perfectly: "It's all over here."

The book, *Catch: A Fishmonger's Guide to Greatness*, is based on the experiences of the crew of a very famous fish market in Seattle called Pike Place Fish. The fish market is a dynamic and exciting environment to visit, but what has made this market stand out from other markets is the set of beliefs that the fishmongers live by. Put simply, they are driven by a desire to make a positive difference to their own lives and the lives of visitors, colleagues and competitors. This philosophy influences the way they act and behave. At Pike Place Fish, the mantra is "It's all over here." This simple statement refers to the principle that all the fishmongers live by, and it means "I am responsible for what I experience and how I react to whatever occurs in my life."

That powerful little statement, "It's all over here," is what all entrepreneurs need to place at the core of everything they do – it means owning your decisions and the outcomes of them. Everything you do starts and finishes with you – no one else. Once you apply this, you will find that even though you will still have numerous difficult situations to deal with, you will not jump to blame others, but rather take personal responsibility and ownership. It will make your life as an entrepreneur more successful, contented and happy!

When you shift your thinking from blame to "It's all over here," fantastic things start to happen for you. What you learn is to accept and realize that everything you think and do is your decision. You start to take responsibility and take back control of everything you do. Not only does that mean that you cope far better with difficult times, as you know you are in control of how you react, but it also means that you can 'create' potential positive outcomes for yourself as you accept "It's all over here." When you understand this, you will find that you react differently to difficult or challenging situations. It does not mean that you will have any less of these, but that you will handle them far better as you accept that everything starts and finishes with you. Blame will be gone – you will be calm, more focused and more in control.

## OBSERVE, LISTEN AND CHAT

Tom's insight on ownership had a big impact on me. It was one of those caddie jobs, like some of the meetings I have as a consultant, that opens up a whole new world of thinking. Tom's off-the-cuff remark led me to write this chapter to illustrate why it is so important for entrepreneurs to understand and apply ownership. At the same time, this story illustrates that you can get insights and wisdom from anywhere – not just from TED Talks, bestselling books or conferences, but in my case from the golf course, the coffee shop or the boardroom.

You can find new insights and wisdom from anywhere that make you a better entrepreneur. All you need to do is to observe, listen to and chat with the many people with whom you will engage during the day. From all of that, someone will say or do something that suddenly sparks an idea or insight that could lead you to a new way of thinking, open up new and exciting opportunities, or help you solve a problem you have been struggling with. All you need to do is to absorb the insight or idea. Trust me, it really is as simple as that to access a world of brilliant, powerful insights and ideas. All you need to do is to say to yourself "It's all over here," and you will find a source that will help you on your way to becoming a successful entrepreneur.

# 8.
# COMPASSION

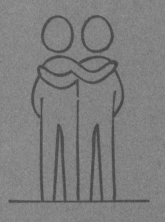

SPORTING CHRIS

# WHY DEMONSTRATE KINDNESS?

I want to introduce you to a social enterprise that is having a massive impact on many people's lives across the UK: Sporting Memories. Have worked with thousands of individuals to date, the enterprise's main purpose is to help people tackle dementia, depression and loneliness through sporting memories. Sporting Memories does this by establishing and running free sporting memories groups for people over the age of 50 across the UK.

By encouraging people to share memories of sporting moments and tap into a passion for sport, Sporting Memories helps people to connect not only with others, but also with their own past, reawakening positive thoughts and feelings that otherwise might remain hidden away. It has been found that these groups have a positive impact on those struggling with dementia, depression and loneliness by increasing their confidence, wellbeing and happiness.

Having mentored Chris Wilkins, one of the co-founders of Sporting Memories, I know him well. Even though I no longer mentor him, we still meet up every now and then for a beer and a catch-up. When we met up last, I was delighted to hear that the business was going from strength to strength. I told Chris that I was delighted for him and the team – I know how much effort and time he has dedicated to the business since he co-founded it in 2011.

He then said something that I thought was fascinating: "Yes, a lot of blood, sweat and tears have been shed over the years, but I now think that we are starting to make a big impact on many people's lives. There have been several times that I felt like walking away, but we made it work."

This intrigued me, and I asked why he hadn't started something else instead.

Chris explained that he had co-founded Sporting Memories because he wanted to combine his passion for sport with helping older people who were isolated and struggling with dementia or depression, or who were simply lonely. He said, "Once you start to help people and you see what a difference it makes to their lives, you can't walk away and let them down."

What Chris was talking about here was **compassion**. And that compassion and kindness extend to how he runs the business for his staff, volunteers, clients and suppliers – acting with compassion and kindness is one of their core values. This has led to a wonderful business that is thriving, growing and helping huge numbers of people.

## COMPASSIONATE ENTREPRENEURSHIP

Chris is a fantastic entrepreneur. He has the passion, creativity, innovation, stamina and belief to have built, from scratch, a thriving business. But at the core of this business is compassion and kindness for others. Now, I know what you might be thinking – that Chris co-founded a business that is not a real business because it is a social enterprise and that his compassion comes from wanting to help others. So, it is easy for Chris to say that compassion and kindness are the core of what he does, but in the real business world, achieving profits must come before anything else.

But is that true? In a 'normal' business, is showing and demonstrating compassion and kindness a 'nice to have' or is it essential for success? In my view, it is fundamental, regardless of what type of business you are running.

If you Google "What makes a great entrepreneur?," you will get roughly the same core traits from several respected websites – passion, creativity, strong work ethic, determination, proactivity, self-motivation, innovation and strong leadership qualities. But never compassion or kindness. These are words not normally associated with entrepreneurship; in fact, most entrepreneurs will probably think that the idea of compassion and kindness seems strange or may even be perceived as weakness. That is because these ideas are synonymous with feelings, empathy, care and the softer side of being human. However, I think entrepreneurs should be actively working towards creating a culture of compassion and kindness that shows care both to themselves and to those they work with. Basically, compassionate entrepreneurship is treating people at work how you would like to be treated.

It makes sense for an entrepreneur to be compassionate, as the benefits can be significant. Treat your staff fairly and with kindness, making sure they feel valued and respected, and they will be more likely to be open with you, share ideas and go that extra mile. A compassionate culture can improve trust, as it allows staff to feel they can raise genuine concerns without fear of reprisal. This can make you a better entrepreneur, and customers who see you as a kind, empathetic and trusting person are more likely to work with you time and time again.

Here is a brilliant quote that sums this up perfectly. It's from Tim Minchin, a comedian, actor and composer, in a speech he made at the University of Western Australia:

*I have, in the past, made important decisions about people I work with – agents and producers – based largely on how they treat wait staff in restaurants. I don't care if you're the most powerful cat in the room, I will judge you on how you treat the least powerful.*

One further, and very important, point is to be compassionate and kind to yourself. You see, if you are kind to yourself, you are more likely to get the balance right between work and play. This could lead you to try to keep fit, eat more healthily and take part in activities you love more often and not focus on work all the time, and all of this can help to reduce the chances of burnout and stress.

## IDEAS ON COMPASSION

Here are a few ideas on how you can start being more compassionate and kind. Trust me, it will make you a better entrepreneur!

- Always try to demonstrate a people-first approach, regardless of whom you are dealing with – whether your staff, customers, suppliers or investors. This means being more transparent, honest and open with everyone.
- Accept that it's okay to make mistakes – in fact, entrepreneurs who are transparent and share their mistakes tend to be more approachable, relatable and human. Don't beat yourself up when you make mistakes or make the wrong decisions.

- Communicate with compassion, wherever possible, and never yell or make unrealistic demands. In every situation, try to communicate with everyone involved, as this encourages commitment and engagement.
- Be driven and motivated by your beliefs, values and purpose and share those with everyone. If you do, then people will not question the motives behind your decisions – instead, they will know that you have considered others rather than focusing on yourself.
- All of this might take courage. You will need to stick to your principles, act ethically and constantly evaluate the impact of your decisions on others. You cannot leave this behaviour to chance – you will need to be proactive in developing compassionate qualities.

Finally, as briefly mentioned above, you need to look after yourself, both mentally and physically, and encourage those you work with to do the same. Give yourself and your staff time during your busy, frantic day to either take part in some physical activity or simply mediate and relax for an hour. You will recoup the rewards in the long term.

For me, the proof in the pudding comes when I look back at all the roles I have undertaken, the companies I have worked for and even the people I have caddied for. It was the people who demonstrated real compassion and kindness towards me that I respected the most.

So, act compassionately as an entrepreneur and you will gain respect, loyalty and a sense of being valued – not a bad thing to gain at all!

# 9.
# LUCK

## THE LUCKY LAWYER

# WHY THREE KEY INGREDIENTS?

When I was young, and until I was in my early thirties, I played rugby. When I started playing the game, my position was either fullback or centre – basically, because I was quite fast and not too overweight, I could beat some opponents for pace and even sometimes sidestep them. However, with the delights of the kebab shops, curry houses and pubs of Edinburgh just on my doorstep, my weight went up, my pace went down and I ended up playing my remaining days of rugby as a number two – the hooker. No longer did I try to outrun or sidestep my opponents – I just tried to run through them, with various levels of success!

I look back on those days with great fondness. Not only did I love playing the game, but I equally enjoyed just being part of such a close-knit team. I got so much out of the training sessions, the captain's pre-match motivational speech, the jugs of beers we drank with our opponents in the clubhouse after the game and just the general banter I had with my teammates. Looking back, the key ingredient that made those rugby days so enjoyable was the experience of comradeship.

Thirty years on, I still find that some of the things I am involved with give me that same feeling of comradeship. And caddying is nearly at the top of the list. You see, if you caddie for someone whose company you enjoy, who is engaging and who is looking for your help and guidance, then you create a bond with that person for four or five hours. They open up to you about their lives, share fascinating and funny stories – and unwittingly give you useful ideas and insights.

And this was exactly what happened when I caddied for Mia from Michigan. Mia had flown in the day before in order to play golf with her son-in-law, who was working in Scotland for the week. They were incorporating a few games of golf around his work commitments.

I was introduced to Mia on the first tee as she walked over to me and shook my hand. She said, "I think we're on deck together" and saluted me with a massive smile. Mia was an incredibly nice woman. Funny, engaging and full of interesting and hilarious stories about some of the clients she had worked for, because it turned out that Mia was a divorce lawyer.

Over the next four or five holes, Mia proceeded to share some of the incredible encounters she had had with some of her clients, as well as thoughts and insights that related well to entrepreneurship. Later, as we were walking down the 11th hole, I continued to chat to her about her successful career as a lawyer. She told me that not only did she have a house in Michigan, but she also had a ski chalet in Vermont and a beach house in South Carolina; in addition, she now worked part time, which allowed her to travel the world.

I said to her that she must have worked very hard to achieve all of this, and she replied with a fascinating answer: "Yes, but do you know what the three key ingredients for real success are? Skill, **luck** and being in the right place at the right time! I had to work hard to get all the qualifications and skills I needed to be a top lawyer, but I also had some luck along the way, and I was in the right place at the right time, which led to work for some excellent clients."

Over the course of our conversation, I realized how important it is to have that point of view in everything you do as an entrepreneur – work hard, know your subject, but don't beat yourself up when things are not going to plan.

## CHRIS, DUSTIN AND MARK

So, let's talk a little bit more about skill, luck and being in the right place at the right time. Let me tell you what is probably one of the best stories that demonstrates this.

I want you to imagine that you are the accommodation officer at Harvard University in the autumn of 2003. The students who enrolled in 2002 have just finished their first year (their freshman year), and they are about to start their second year. As the accommodation officer, you run a computer programme that allocates these students to their rooms for the second year. Next to you, the printer jumps into life and prints out the lists showing which students are allocated to which rooms. You then take the printed sheets for the various dorms and houses and you give them to your staff. During the day, all the second-year students arrive and find out which rooms they have been allocated. In room H33, three people find that they are going to be living together for their second year. They are Chris Hughes, Dustin Moskovitz and Mark Zuckerberg – the co-founders of Facebook.

That computer programme that randomly put Hughes, Moskovitz and Zuckerberg together helped to start one of the biggest companies in the world today. Had Hughes or Moskovitz been allocated to another room and two other people been allocated to room H33, would Facebook have existed? I have no idea.

Zuckerberg is obviously an incredibly clever and skilful computer programmer. However, the chemistry between Hughes, Moskovitz and Zuckerberg, and the ideas that they must have bounced around in that room about a social media platform, were also crucial. Because they were allocated to room H33, today Hughes, Moskovitz and Zuckerberg are millionaires or billionaires. They have changed the way in which we all communicate and share details of our lives. They have inspired so many other entrepreneurs. And this is all down in some way to luck and being in the right place at the right time.

As Hughes acknowledges in his book, *Fair Shot: Rethinking Inequality and How We Earn*:

> *Saying people get lucky is not a denial that they work hard and deserve positive outcomes. It is a way of acknowledging that in a winner-take-all economy, small, chance encounters – like who you sit down next to at a dinner party or who your college roommate is – have a more significant impact than they have ever had before. In some cases, the collections of these small differences can add up to create immense fortunes.*

There are so many similar stories that I just love. For example, would Apple have even existed if Steve Jobs had not met Steve Wozniak? The reason they met was down to one of Apple's earliest employees, Bill Fernandez. It was Fernandez who was responsible for introducing them back in 1971, long before Apple was formed. Back then, Fernandez was friends with both Wozniak and Jobs separately. One day, Fernandez was walking around the neighbourhood with Jobs when he saw Wozniak outside washing his car.

This was the perfect opportunity, he thought, to introduce the two to each other. He figured they would get along because they shared a love of technology and playing pranks. Jobs and Wozniak hit it off immediately and, before long, they started hanging out together on their own, without Fernandez. They would work together on practical jokes and tech projects, and soon they started working together professionally, too. That then led to the formation of Apple and the rest is history.

So, if Jobs had not gone for a walk with Fernandez that day in his neighbourhood, would Jobs have met Wozniak some other way? If Wozniak had not decided to wash his car and had stayed inside, would they have met? I have no idea! But the fact that Jobs and Wozniak did meet that day – and eventually founded Apple – was partly down to them being in the right place at the right time and some luck.

## DON'T BEAT YOURSELF UP

So why am I telling you these stories? Well, from my own personal experience and from that of many people I have met, all entrepreneurs have stories about how close they have been to that 'event' that could have taken them to the next major stage of their business. Such events might be getting that big investment they need to develop their product further, landing that new client who will provide them with a six-figure annual contract, or receiving that government grant that will allow them to employ a new team – but the event just doesn't happen. So the entrepreneur gets frustrated and stressed, and doesn't understand why things are not working out. They work incredibly hard, believe passionately in what they are trying to achieve, are motivated, have a great team around them and make personal sacrifices in order to try to make their business successful. They have read all the books that promise to tell them how to be a successful entrepreneur, they have attended conferences (at great expense!) to listen to 'industry experts', and they have sacrificed evenings and weekends to attend networking events hoping to make 'that connection'. But still, things are not working out for them. And so, the entrepreneur starts to feel beaten.

If that has happened to you (it has certainly happened to me), then try and think like this: *right now, luck is not on your side and you have not yet met the person, or the opportunity, that will take your business to the next stage. However, you know you have the skills and knowledge to be a success. So dust yourself down, continue with what you believe in, stick to your values and remember the purpose that initially drove you to become an entrepreneur. The three key ingredients for success will come together one day – specifically, your luck will change, you will be in the right place at the right time, and you will be able to apply all your skills and knowledge to the new opportunities that come your way. It will happen!*

It is all about those three key ingredients.

# 10.
# FAILURE

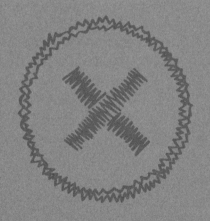

## LESSONS FROM
## EDINBURGH

# WHY DO YOU NEED TO FAIL?

I love living near and working in Edinburgh. It is a beautiful, historic and vibrant city. It has fantastic architecture, from the imposing castle to Holyrood Palace to the stunning Georgian New Town, to name just a few well-known landmarks. There are wonderful art galleries, bars, restaurants and hotels. And every year in July and August, Edinburgh hosts six festivals, the biggest being the Edinburgh Fringe. During this time, the population of Edinburgh doubles, which is great for the hospitality businesses based in Edinburgh, but not for others trying to live in or get around the city!

Edinburgh has also now become the centre of entrepreneurial start-up companies in the UK. In 2016, Edinburgh won the Entrepreneurial City of the Year award at the Great British Entrepreneur Awards, beating Cambridge, London and Manchester. There are several start-up incubators, such as Entrepreneurial Spark and Codebase, where companies are offered office space, mentoring and networking opportunities. In addition, every year there is a conference called EIE (Engage Invest Exploit) where start-up companies get the opportunity to pitch to many investors. In 2017, the conference was held at the Edinburgh International Conference Centre.

I have been attending EIE for many years, and 2017 was an excellent event. Some great start-ups were pitching, and there were excellent networking opportunities and four good keynote speakers. The speech that I found the most useful was given by the CEO and founder of RocketSpace, Duncan Logan. RocketSpace is an incubator based in San Francisco that supports more than 1,000 high-growth start-ups and corporate innovators. His speech took the format of an interview with the BBC journalist Clare English, who asked him several questions about RocketSpace and the world of start-ups. It was a fascinating interview, but the stand-out part for me was when English asked Logan whether UK and US entrepreneurs have different mindsets in relation to start-ups. She observed that it seemed to her that US start-ups embrace failure because they view it as the next step to success, whereas entrepreneurs in the UK see failure as a bad thing. And this is how Logan responded:

*The stats about this are fascinating: 90% of first-time founders will **fail**; 80% will never try again. But those that do try again, the numbers flip. In your second business, 90% of those who tried again will be successful.*

This was intriguing to hear, and I do think it is true. Entrepreneurs in the US do embrace failure – they are not put off by it. They learn from their failure, dust themselves down and start again. However, the mindsets of UK entrepreneurs are gradually changing. I have met and worked with several start-up entrepreneurs based in Edinburgh, and their philosophy around failure is becoming more in tune with what Logan and English were saying. Many of these entrepreneurs whose original idea 'failed' did try again and are now running successful businesses.

The day after the conference, I had a meeting with an investor, Rebecca, and during our meeting we discussed Logan's theory and the statistics he provided. Rebecca totally agreed with what Duncan had said and added that she wished some of the companies that she had invested in would 'pivot'.

"Pivot?" I asked "What on earth do you mean by that?"

She laughed at my response and told me to get with the trendy start-up lingo!

"'Pivot' means the business is having to change its strategy, and it's a much better word for an investor to hear than 'flopped'," she said and burst out laughing.

So, whatever you call it – changing course, pivoting or flopping – any successful entrepreneur needs to embrace failure because there is so much more to learn from failure than from success.

## FAILURE AND SUCCESS

Looking back on my own entrepreneurial career, I can honestly say that it is the failures rather than the successes that have taught me more about myself, my business and my co-workers. The experience and knowledge you gain when you encounter failure can be harnessed in the future to help you be successful in the long term.

Failure also builds resilience. For some, the more you fail, the more resilient you will become. And to achieve great success, you need to be resilient because success rarely happens on the first attempt. As Duncan highlighted, only 10% of first-time founders will try again after they have failed the first time around. It is a very painful process to go through when you fail in business – your pride and self-confidence are normally hit hard. People whom you have employed lose their jobs. Suppliers to your business might not get paid. And your customers' orders for products or services are not fulfilled. So, while it takes courage and self-belief to pick yourself back up after a failure, it is your resilience that keeps you moving forward to trying again (and again!). Resilience gets rid of the lofty expectation that things will happen overnight, and in comes the expectation that true success will take an enormous amount of work and effort.

Failure also helps you grow and mature as an entrepreneur. It helps you to challenge your purpose and beliefs about what you are trying to achieve. This helps you to reflect and put things into perspective, developing meaning from the painful situations that you go through. As long as you can identify why you failed, failure can be a brilliant teacher to help you not to make the same mistakes again.

Finally, failure also teaches you to value success. If you have gone through periods of failure as an entrepreneur, then when success comes, you will not take it for granted. You will feel that you have really earned your success when you reflect on the dark days, when nothing was going right for you. There is nothing better than achieving success if you have gone through periods of failure to get there. It is these failures that can help you to become a better entrepreneur.

## HARRY POTTER

At the start of this chapter, I listed some of Edinburgh's wonderful landmarks, festivals and start-up communities. But one recent Edinburgh resident who encapsulates everything I mean about embracing failure is the author of the Harry Potter series, J. K. Rowling. For me, Rowling is one of the most inspirational success stories of our time. Many people probably know her simply as the woman who created Harry Potter. But what most people don't know is that she experienced many years of 'failure' and struggle before she achieved worldwide fame.

It was back in 1990 that Rowling first had the idea for Harry Potter. She has related how the idea came fully formed into her mind one day while she was on a train from Manchester to London. She began writing furiously. In 1993, her first marriage ended in divorce, so she moved to Edinburgh to be closer to her sister. In her suitcase were three chapters of Harry Potter.

Rowling saw herself as a failure at this time. She was jobless, divorced and penniless and had a dependent child. She suffered with bouts of depression, eventually signing up for government welfare. It was a difficult time in her life, but she pushed through the failures, continuing to write using the coffee shops of Edinburgh as her base.

In 1995, she sent the manuscript of her first Harry Potter book to 12 major publishers. They all rejected it. But she continued to believe some publisher would pick it up. And they did – later that year, Bloomsbury accepted it and extended her a very small £1,500 advance. In 1997, the book was published with a print run of only 1,000 copies, 500 of which were distributed to libraries. In 1997 and 1998, the book won the Nestlé Smarties Book Prize and the British Book Awards Children's Book of the Year. After all that failure, Rowling had an explosion of success. Today, she has sold more than 400 million copies of her books and is the most successful female author in the UK. She has achieved worldwide recognition.

In 2008, Rowling was asked to give the commencement speech at Harvard University to those graduating that year. It was a brilliant speech and a big part of it was about her experiences of failure:

> *The knowledge that you have emerged wiser and stronger from setbacks means that you are, ever after, secure in your ability to survive. You will never truly know yourself, or the strength of your relationships, until both have been tested by adversity. Such knowledge is a true gift, for all that it is painfully won, and it has been worth more than any qualification I ever earned.*

So, as you are going forward as an entrepreneur, take a leaf out of the book of one of the most successful authors in the world about failure and embrace it. When success eventually does arrive, you will be wiser, stronger, more grateful and much more resilient.

# 11.
# TRUST

TWO BIG EARS

# WHY TRUST IN THE DOTS?

One of first challenges you will encounter as an entrepreneur is what to call your new venture or business. It might be very obvious, and you might settle on a name very quickly. Or you might choose to talk to people whom you trust and get their ideas.

Over the years, I have attended many events and conferences where start-up businesses were either looking for advice or pitching for new investment. I sometimes have to smile at the names entrepreneurs choose for their new business. Looking back, at least half the names I've encountered made no sense, weren't proper words or didn't in the least reflect what the business was all about.

I can remember one such workshop where ten start-ups were looking for advice and mentoring. The workshop was being run by the University of Edinburgh and I, along with several other seasoned entrepreneurs, had been invited to come and listen to a ten-minute pitch by each of the ten start-ups about their business or idea. We were then asked to give our feedback on the pitch.

I have done several of these workshops and I enjoy them, but the reason this particular workshop sticks in my mind is the name of one of the start-ups. It is without doubt the best name I have heard for a business. This start-up designed interactive audio applications and its founders saw their markets as being in both the mobile and the gaming sectors. The name of the start-up was Two Big Ears. What a great name for a business that focuses on cutting-edge audio technology – it is memorable, clever and fun, and it explains exactly what the company does. Who wouldn't want to buy something from a business with the name Two Big Ears?

I said as much when the two founders, Abesh Thakur and Varun Nair, had finished their pitch. I thought they potentially had a great product and asked whether they wanted to meet up for a coffee at another time, so I could give them more specific advice and suggestions. They were delighted with my offer and two weeks later we met in Browns, a café in Edinburgh.

We had a good discussion about their business and the product, and hopefully I gave them sound advice. I was about to wrap up the meeting when the person whom I was meeting next, Peter, arrived early. I decided that it would be a good idea to introduce Peter to Abesh and Varun, as Peter was the CEO of a digital agency and would understand the potential opportunity that Two Big Ears' technology offered. By the end of that introductory chat, Abesh and Varun had been offered free office space in Peter's agency and promised introductions to people in the tech world, as well as to several individuals who could help with the business.

At the end of the meeting, I shook the hands of Abesh and Varun and commented that the meeting had gone far better than I expected. It is not often you offer to help a start-up and an hour later its founders have been offered free office space, introductions to potential clients, and general support – and I did nothing other than invite Peter to join us! The guys were incredibly grateful for the meeting and I wished them all the best for the future.

Over the next six months, I heard from various sources that Two Big Ears was growing and had got some investment. Abesh and Varun had appointed an experienced chairman and non-executive director, and were now working with some great clients. They were also still in Peter's office.

Around 18 months after that meeting, I got a call from Peter saying that Two Big Ears had been bought by Facebook in a great deal for all involved.

# RANDOM EVENTS

Now, you may be wondering what on earth this story has to do with the question "Why trust in the dots?" Well, the story illustrates the issue of **trust**, which is a fundamental requirement for every entrepreneur. There are various types of trust – trust in your staff, trust of family and friends, and trust of clients. And these are all important. But, as an entrepreneur, you must also have trust in yourself.

Trusting in yourself is far more than trusting your idea, your business plan or your strategy. All of this is good, and all of this is important, but you must also trust that all the effort you are making, the meetings you go to and the events you attend will eventually help you to achieve your goals. And it is also about trusting that when things get tough, or when you seem to be stuck, or when you feel your entrepreneurial career is going backwards, you will come out the other side and positive things will emerge. At the time, you won't be able to see what those positive things will be, but you must trust that things will turn out for the best at some point in the future.

The best way to clarify and illustrate what I mean is to share a story about Steve Jobs. Jobs, for me, explains this idea of trusting in yourself perfectly.

My guess is that some of you reading this book will have watched Jobs's commencement speech at Stanford University in 2005. If you haven't, get your computer, search for the speech, sit back and enjoy! I hope you'll agree with me – it is a brilliant speech. One of the most powerful parts of the speech is when Jobs talks about 'connecting the dots'. 'Dots', from Jobs's perspective, are random events that don't initially seem to be connected. In the speech, he uses the example of himself, at the age of 17, dropping out of college after only six months, but being allowed to 'drop into' other classes that he was interested in.

One of those classes was calligraphy. He was inspired by the class and what it taught him about beauty and design. However, although he really enjoyed the class, he felt that it would probably be of no use in later life. But, as he explained in his speech, ten years later, when he was designing the first Mac, he remembered how inspired he had been by the calligraphy class. Based on that experience, he decided that his new Mac would use multiple typefaces and proportionally spaced fonts. He wanted fonts on the Mac to be beautiful and offer choice. Up to that point, all personal computer fonts had been ugly and boring and used the same typeface. Those seemingly disconnected events – Jobs dropping out of college, taking a calligraphy class, and then building and designing the Mac – helped to change personal computing for the better and made the Mac into one of the best computers in the world.

Jobs concluded that part of his speech with this brilliant observation about random events in life:

> *You can't connect the dots looking forward; you can only connect them looking backwards. So, you have to trust*

*that the dots will somehow connect in your future.*
*You have to trust in something – your gut, destiny, life,*
*karma, whatever. This approach has never let me down,*
*and it has made all the difference in my life.*

Basically, what Steve was saying is to trust in yourself. You are the only one who knows where you are going, even though it might not be that obvious at the time. It is only when you get there that you can connect the dots that got you to your goal.

As an entrepreneur, you will have good days and bad days. There will be meetings that are disastrous or pointless. There will be pitches you win and pitches you lose. You might go for investment confident in your business plan only to find that it is rejected. At the time, you probably won't give a second thought to how these experiences could have an impact on you later on, but somewhere down the line some of these random events, meetings and situations could one day turn out to be connected. These random events (dots in your life) could take you to real success and open up a whole new world of opportunities. And it is all about trusting in yourself to continue to do things that you believe in and that give you purpose. Then, one day in the future, you can look back and say, "Ah, now I can see how I have got to where I am."

So, let's go back to Two Big Ears. When I heard that Facebook had bought Two Big Ears, I emailed Abesh to congratulate him and Varun, and I received a lovely email back that sums up perfectly how seemingly random events and meetings (dots) may connect together:

*We [Abesh and Varun] quite often like to discuss how that
meeting in Browns led us to many more introductions
and was one of the many serendipitous events
that led to this day.*

## LOOKING BACK

If you had said to me just after my stroke that 11 years on I would
have written two books, I would have thought you insane. But that
is what has happened. When I look back now, I can see what, at
the time, must have seemed like random events (dots):

- A friend suggested I watch a TED Talk titled "My Stroke of Insight" by Jill Bolte Taylor, which I did.
- I watched a film called *The Diving Bell and the Butterfly*,
which is about life after a stroke, and then straight afterwards bought and read the book the film is based on, by
Jean-Dominique Bauby.
- I switched on the TV and watching a programme with my wife
about the caddies at St Andrews golf course. Based on that
programme, she suggested I should think about caddying, as
it might help my recovery from my stroke.
- I went to see the caddie master at North Berwick Golf Club
and, even though my confidence was at its lowest because of
the effects of the stroke, he gave me my first caddie job.
- I did hundreds of 'random' caddie jobs where I met many interesting and fascinating people.

Now, looking back, I can see how all these random events became connected. The inspirational TED Talk showed me that
good things could come from my stroke as long as I gave it time;

Jean-Dominique Bauby's book (and the film that was made of it) showed me that even someone who had had a horrific stroke could write a book; watching the TV programme about St Andrews inspired my wife to suggest I become a caddie; the caddie master supported and actively encouraged me to be a caddie; and the people I met caddying inspired me with their stories. Then, one day, I came home from caddying and said to my family, "I am going to write a book about starting again based on all my experiences as a CEO, stroke survivor and caddie." I can now look back and see how everything that led me to write my first book and now this one was connected.

So, trust in yourself. Each time you attend a terrible meeting, have a pitch go badly or get denied funding for your business, just trust that all these seemingly random events will one day connect together to give you entrepreneurial success.

And you never know: Facebook might be in touch!

# 12.
# COPY

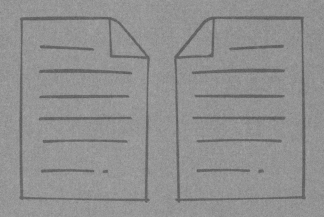

THE FRENCH THIEF

# WHY DO YOU NEED TO STEAL?

I have a strange relationship with France and the French. One of my best holidays was in Paris, but my worst holiday ever was in Bordeaux. One of my favourite restaurants in Edinburgh is French, but one of the worst bouts of food poisoning I have had was when I ate in a bistro in Nice. I admire greatly the independent spirit of the French, yet I get incredibly annoyed with them when one of their strikes affects my holiday!

This relationship with the French extends to caddying. Out of all the caddying jobs I have done over the years, some of the most difficult have been for French people, but so have some of the most enjoyable. You just don't know which Frenchman or French-woman is going to turn up!

Fortunately, when I met Philippe from Normandy on the first tee, I sensed this was definitely going to be a good French experience. He was very welcoming and seemed to be enormously excited about playing golf at North Berwick, "I just love this course," he said. "This is my fifth visit to play on it." Then he hit a brilliant drive, splitting the fairway.

And my intuition was correct. Philippe was incredibly friendly and chatty, and also a very good golfer – no looking for balls in the rough for me! This all boded well, as Philippe was playing golf on his own and there is nothing worse than caddying for a single player who doesn't want to talk or doesn't ask for your advice! As we walked along the second hole, I asked him what he did for a living, and to my surprise he told me that he owned and ran a golf course in Normandy.

I was intrigued and asked whether he had bought it from someone, but he went on to explain that he had managed the designing and building of the course himself ten years ago. He told me that because of his love for the North Berwick golf course, he had copied holes 15 and 16 in the design of his own course. "Absolutely brilliant holes," he said.

I have to agree that those holes are great. The 15th hole, called Redan, is the most copied par three in the world, and the 16th green is one of the most challenging you will ever play – trust me, I have had so many rounds of golf destroyed on that hole when I've played it!

"Is that what you did with the other holes you designed on your course?" I asked.

"Yes," Phillipe replied. "I travelled and visited many golf courses both in Europe and America, stealing ideas from different holes that I could then incorporate into my course. And I think that philosophy worked out really well, as I have what I think is a wonderful golf course that I love. But I am biased. If you're ever in Normandy, you should come and play – you can compare my 16th hole with your 16th hole." He laughed and then hit a superb shot into the middle of the fifth green.

## COPY, COPY, COPY!

Phillipe's habit of copying or stealing is a great habit to foster and use time and time again as an entrepreneur. Obviously, I am not actually suggesting you physically copy or steal a patented idea or something similar – that would not be good advice! When I say 'steal', I mean what Austin Kleon says in his brilliant book *Steal Like an Artist*:

*Start **copying** what you love. Copy, copy, copy, copy.*
*At the end of the copy you will find yourself.*

That quote Kleon 'stole' from the Japanese fashion designer, Yohji Yamamoto!

That is what Philippe did to build a golf course that he now loves – he copied. He copied the bits of other golf courses he either admired or was passionate about, and then took all these ideas back to Normandy and built his course – a course he was incredibly proud of.

As an entrepreneur, you must get into the habit of doing this all the time. The more you copy or 'steal' what you see as examples of success, the more likely you are to become successful. It's obvious, really – copy the things you admire, copy the things you really like, copy the habits of entrepreneurs you look up to, copy ideas you love from TED Talks, copy insights from books that inspire you, and copy bits of wisdom from films and TV programmes that fuel your imagination. Basically, copy anything that resonates with you and that will help you to become a better and more effective entrepreneur. And, when you copy, remember that the chances are that you will improve the thing you are copying! As Kleon says:

*All creative works build on what came before.*
*Nothing is completely original.*

It is crucial, though, to distinguish, as Kleon highlights, what is good and bad theft. 'Bad theft' is to plagiarize, imitate, rip off and steal from only one source. 'Good theft' is to credit, honour, transform and steal from many.

You might think that becoming an author is not a very entrepreneurial thing to do. Well, if you think that, I have to tell you that you're wrong! If you are to have any chance of being a successful author these days, you need to see your book as a business. Not only do you need to come up with the core idea of your book, but you also need a structure for every chapter, and then you need to write the book – and that's the easy bit! To have any chance of success, you need a full marketing strategy in place – for pre-launch, launch and post-launch – and then you need to implement it. Yep, authorship is a business, normally a solo one, and I believe you need a real entrepreneurial spirit to make a book successful.

I see myself as an 'entrepreneurial author', and do you know one of the things that really helped me to write and get my two books published? I stole!

I have a great friend, whom I admire enormously, who is one of the people I 'steal' and copy ideas from. Don't worry, I have told him. He constantly sends out emails and Facebook updates with inspiring thoughts, links to resources he thinks people will find useful and videos of inspiring people. When I wrote my first book and then this book, I am happy to say that some of the ideas and insights came from him. I stole them! Without these ideas, my book would have been far more difficult to write. So, I copied ideas for both my books from other authors, used quotes from famous people I admire, used Google constantly, and had lunches or beers with other entrepreneurs, authors, businesspeople, peers and friends who gave me stories, insights or ideas. I caddied for people like Phillipe, who gave some of my chapters brilliant little stories and helped me to illustrate a point I wanted to make. I studied successful book launches; I followed authors who were very active on Facebook, LinkedIn and Twitter; and I went to book festivals to listen to authors talks and see how they communicated with their audience. In all of these ways, I tried to copy the things other people did that seemed to make them more successful.

## THE FOSBURY FLOP AND JACK
But don't take my word for it – just look at the world of sport.

In between bouts of writing this book, I watched the 2016 Rio Olympics. The events were fantastic to watch – inspiring, motivational and hugely enjoyable. One of the most competitive events I watched was the women's heptathlon high jump, which ended up as a battle between Jessica Ennis-Hill, Katarina Johnson-Thompson and Nafissatou Thiam. It was a great event, with Thiam eventually jumping the highest and winning the event.

And do you know what was one of the main reasons why Ennis-Hill, Johnson-Thompson and Thiam achieved excellent results? Indeed, all three achieved personal bests. The answer is that they copied! You see, in the history of the high jump, for a long time the athletes really only used two techniques to try to jump over the bar: firstly the 'scissors technique' and then the 'straddle'. But, in the 1968 Olympics, an American high-jumper called Richard Fosbury revolutionized the high-jump event with a unique 'back-first' technique. It was such a successful technique that nearly all high-jumpers since have copied it, to the extent that it is now called the 'Fosbury flop'. By copying Fosbury's technique, Ennis-Hill, Johnson-Thompson and Thiam jumped far higher than it would have been possible to do with other techniques. Copying made them better athletes.

Still not convinced? Okay, let me give you another example. Back to the world of golf!

Most people agree that one the world's greatest golfers, if not the greatest golfer ever, is Jack Nicklaus. Among many things he possesses as a golfer is a fantastic golf swing. One thing Nicklaus does with his golf swing is that he turns his head slightly to the right just before he starts his swing. Nicklaus believes that this slight action makes all the difference to his swing. Based on Nicklaus's success, many golfers have copied that technique. However, it turns out that Nicklaus didn't originate the move – in fact, he borrowed it from another very famous golfer, Sam Snead. Snead won seven major golf competitions in the 1940s and the 1950s. As Nicklaus said in an article for *GolfDigest* magazine in 2011:

*Turning the head was something I saw Sam Snead do when I played an exhibition with him at age 16 between the second and third rounds of the Ohio State Open. I figured if it was good enough for Sam, it was good enough for me.*

So there you go: long before Nicklaus was the greatest golfer ever, he copied a move from one of the best golfers of the day, Sam Snead. Copying worked pretty well for Nicklaus – he has won more major golf competitions (18) than any other golfer in the world. Trust me, the top sportspeople, the most successful sports teams, the most innovative businesses and the best entrepreneurs copy. They take the best ideas, techniques, theories and insights and they copy them in some way. Sometimes they just imitate them. Other times they copy and then improve the thing they have copied. Sometimes, they copy a small thing that does not fundamentally change what they were doing already, but that could give them a little edge against their competitors. But sometimes, they see something so fundamentally different, something so much better, that it would be madness not to copy it.

So, as an entrepreneur, you really need to get into a habit of stealing. And do you know what is one of the best compliments any entrepreneur can get? That other entrepreneurs start to steal your ideas, insights and techniques!

# 13.
# LONELINESS

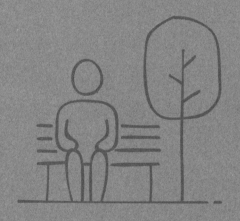

CRYING IN PUBLIC

# WHY WILL YOU BE LONELY?

Now, I am not ashamed to admit that one of the perks that I enjoyed as a CEO was when I was invited to what is known in the business circles as 'corporates'. Corporates tend to be either sporting or cultural events – for example, Six Nations rugby, Premier League football, a rock concert or a book festival. Usually, it is a supplier or (sometimes) a client who invites you.

One of the most memorable ones was when I was invited to the Wimbledon semi-finals by one of my company's major clients. As well as me, the client had invited a few other suppliers to the event. One of the other suppliers invited was Paul (for confidentiality reasons I am using a pseudonym), the CEO of an advertising company whom I had worked with in the past. I had always admired Paul because he had built up a very successful business that had offices in various locations. He just seemed to be a nice guy, who was well respected both in advertising circles and in business generally. There had been a lot of articles in the press about his business and how successful it was. It was great to have a quick chat with Paul, but we all wanted to see the tennis, so we agreed to meet after the tennis had concluded, for a meal at an Italian restaurant Paul knew, to have a proper catch-up.

It was great to find out what had been going on with Paul and that the press articles were correct. Business was booming. His company had won some major new clients and was having its best financial year ever, and Paul had built a great leadership team around himself. Envious, me ... ? Never! We then had a chat about how my business was faring, and although I could not claim the same level of success, I told him that things were going in a very positive direction.

We then started to talk about some of the challenges we were both facing as CEOs, mainly focusing on staff and client issues. And then (maybe it was the wine talking), Paul asked me a very profound question, a question I had never been asked before during my time as a CEO.

"Do you get **lonely** as a CEO?" Paul asked.

"Lonely?" I replied. "What do you mean?"

"Well, don't you find being a CEO is a very lonely position to be in? On one side, you have all your staff and clients and then on the other side the other directors, the chairman and your shareholders. And as the CEO you sit in between them all ... on your own."

When Paul said that it was like a lightbulb switching on in my head. The more I thought about it, the more I started to realize that being a CEO was indeed a very lonely position.

Having thought about it a little more, I told Paul I agreed with him. I told him how I had a great leadership team, a good chairman, loyal staff and a very supportive family, but at the end of the day there was nobody I could actually talk to about the challenges of being the CEO, as none of them had experienced it. So yes, I realized that I did get lonely. Although I had not been asked to articulate the feeling as loneliness before, this was the best description I had heard to date. Then, as we continued to talk, Paul burst into tears!

Now, this was the last thing I expected. Here I was sitting in a lovely restaurant watching Paul, one of the most successful CEOs I knew, crying. But I could really relate to why he was crying – he was lonely. But it is a specific type of loneliness that CEOs and entrepreneurs will experience and suffer sometime in their career – sometimes more than once. It is that they have no one to talk to about their toughest challenges, their fears and their worries in what they do day after day.

## LONELY AT THE TOP

As an entrepreneur, this feeling of isolation will be one of the biggest challenges you will have to face. The accepted and expected 'public face' of a successful entrepreneur should ooze confidence, control, decisiveness and direction, to clients, staff, other directors, shareholders and investors. Therefore, it is understandable that any entrepreneur could find it difficult to talk with key staff or their boards about their biggest problems and deepest fears. You don't want to appear vulnerable.

As an entrepreneur who wants to be successful, it is likely that you will employ many people, work with lots of clients, attend lots of meetings, be asked to read many reports and proposals, and seem to be constantly on the phone. And there lies the real paradox: despite being surrounded by loads of people who work for you and having whole teams at your beck and call, you will sometimes feel terribly alone. You may be always busy, in constant demand and interacting with other people, but this will give you a false sense of being connected. Trust me, you will have plenty of people to talk to, but few with whom you can really share the deep concerns, frustrations and challenges that you are facing.

And it's this inability to share what you are really feeling that can create a huge sense of isolation.

It can also be difficult to socialize with colleagues who work for you. Everyone is on their best behaviour when they go out with the boss! Friendship and chumminess at a rugby game or at the bar can often feel strained and false.

But what about the entrepreneurs who don't want to build a company? Those who prefer working on their own – the solo entrepreneurs? Solo entrepreneurs in the main run their business from home – usually in a dedicated space. There is the same problem, though – a feeling of isolation and loneliness, but with different challenges. This time the loneliness is mainly caused by limited opportunities to interact with others. When solo entrepreneurs make a coffee in the morning, there is no prospect of bumping into someone in the office kitchen with whom you can have an informal chat. When they go and grab a sandwich at lunch time, they will not meet other people from the company. And when they have an idea or a problem they can't solve, they can't just walk into someone's office and chat it through. All of this, and more, can make for a very lonely scenario.

The problem with both of these scenarios – the entrepreneurs who work with many people and the solo entrepreneurs – is serious. If it's not managed, this feeling of loneliness can manifest as real frustration that starts to affect not only your performance as an entrepreneur, but also your personal relationships and your health.

Certainly, when I was a CEO, I did experience loneliness. Don't get me wrong, there were many brilliant benefits to being an entrepreneurial CEO, and for me they outweighed the downsides. But one of the downsides was definitely loneliness – the feeling that, at the end of the day, you have no one you can really open up to and have a completely honest discussion with about your fears, your weaknesses and the pressures you are under.

That meal with Paul crystallized some things in my mind. I can remember coming home, many times, and trying to articulate what I was feeling to my wife. I certainly was not lonely in my personal relationship – my wife was, and still is, incredibly supportive in everything I do. But she found it very difficult to understand my feeling of isolation as a CEO – not because she was not empathetic, but because my challenges and problems as an entrepreneurial CEO were unique to me. Sometimes, when I felt lonely and like no one understood the real pressures I was under, who did I vent my frustration on? My poor wife!

And how did I try to manage that loneliness? Booze. I have never been one of those people who go to the pub on a regular basis. Even though I enjoy meeting friends over a few pints, my drinking was done at home. Having a drink as soon as I walked through the door was a habit I perfected when I was a CEO. Not only did I feel I 'deserved' it, but it was also the thing that, for a while, relieved me of my feeling of isolation and frustration. And that's fine if it stays at one or two drinks. Sometimes it stopped there, but other nights it quickly grew to three or four and maybe even more. And do you know something – the feeling of loneliness and frustration that had built up over the day initially disappeared after that first drink, but it came back even stronger if I continued to drink, and then who was in the firing range? My family!

Now, I hope you'll see that this is a difficult thing for me to put into print, but I think it is very important to understand. The effects of loneliness on you and how you cope with it as an entrepreneur will be very challenging if you don't have strategies and ideas on how to manage it. I eventually worked out what those strategies and ideas were with lots of help, but not before I had caused too many arguments and drunk more whisky than I should have!

## TALK, TALK, TALK

So, whether you are an entrepreneur employing many staff and with a board to report to or whether you are going to remain as a solo entrepreneur, let me suggest the following ideas to help you manage your loneliness.

It is all about building a team around you that you trust. The first and most fundamental thing is that you have someone who you can talk to openly and regularly who is already a proven entrepreneur. That does not necessary mean that they have been successful – in fact, entrepreneurs who have tasted real business failure can prove to be really helpful. I would call this person your mentor or coach. This is an individual you will meet on a regular basis – a minimum of once a month – to talk and share your concerns and thoughts about your progress as an entrepreneur. Where do you find these mentors and coaches, you might ask? One source is networking events, or you could identify entrepreneurs you really admire in business and approach them, meet up with them over a coffee or lunch, and see whether there is real chemistry between you. If there is, then meet them a few times more and then ask whether they are willing to be your mentor or coach. Obviously, you will need to pay for this, but from my experience, it is one of the best investments you will ever make.

Secondly, join an entrepreneurs' group. If you are unaware of where to find such a group, just Google 'entrepreneurs' group' and you will find many listed. Over the past ten years, a variety of entrepreneurs' networks have been set up. Also known as 'entrepreneurs' peer groups', they typically consist of eight to twelve entrepreneurs who get together for frank discussions on how they can better manage their businesses and, often, their lives. These groups normally meet a minimum of six times per year and each meeting can last anywhere from half a day to a full day. They provide an excellent forum in which to talk and discuss the big challenges you are facing as an entrepreneur. You will get fantastic advice and guidance, as well as being able to help other entrepreneurs in the group. These groups will often have a guest speaker, again someone to whom you will be able to relate. Over the years, I have attended a number of these groups, and they are excellent. Yes, you will have to give up a day of your time, but, again, it is absolutely worth it in the long term.

Going back to Paul, I shared this advice with him and he took it on board. When I saw him last, he thanked me over lunch for introducing him to one of these groups, which is based in Scotland. He said he was incredibly embarrassed about crying in public, but he also said it had been the tipping point that had made him realize he had to get some outside help. I told him he did not need to feel embarrassed at all – it is something I have done many times!

# 14.
# PERSPECTIVE

## THE WISE
## UNDERTAKER

# WHY BOOK A MEETING AT THE GYM?

One of the great joys of caddying is that you meet a wide range of people from different parts of the world. One day you might be caddying for a marketing director from Seattle, the next an architect from Japan. One of the strange habits I have got into when I am caddying is that I try to guess the occupation of the person for whom I am caddying.

Obviously, I keep this habit to myself, but from the moment I am introduced to the person on the first tee and as we walk up the first fairway chatting, I am trying to work out what this person does for a living. But do you know something? I am rubbish at it! People I initially think are CEOs of large companies turn out to be doctors, doctors turn out to be plumbers and plumbers turn out to be sportspeople. But it keeps me entertained!

The day I caddied for George from Chicago, I could have spent the whole round trying to guess his occupation, but I would never have got it right. I initially though he was either a venture capitalist or a corporate lawyer. In fact, I was so convinced that I was going to be right this time that I decided I would reveal what I thought he did before either I asked him or he volunteered it. On the first tee, George had introduced himself by telling me that he was from Chicago.

I had done some work there about 12 years ago and loved the place. One thing that had struck me was that all the bars and restaurants I had gone to were packed with businesspeople, all wearing smart suits and outfits. They all looked like very successful corporate lawyers or people in finance, and so I asked George whether he was a lawyer.

George laughed out loud and said, "Lawyer ... me, no, not all. I'm an undertaker! I've buried many lawyers over my career, but have never been one."

So, wrong again!

George told me he had been working as an undertaker for 30 years. Like a great entrepreneur, he had started at the bottom of the rung by initially digging the graves during his apprenticeship and over the years he had decided to set up his own undertaking business, which had turned out to be very successful. He told me that he'd sold his business the previous year and was now enjoying retirement – playing lots of golf!

George turned out to be one of the most lovely, gentle and calm people I have ever caddied for. He was an average golfer, but whether he hit a great shot or a poor one, his reaction was always the same – patience, calmness and acceptance. He would just move on to the next shot, and whatever the outcome was he didn't get stressed or angry over a poor shot or too elated over a great one.

I finally decided to say to George that he was one of the most relaxed golfers I had ever caddied for and that I wished some of the others had had the same attitude as him.

Smiling, George turned to me and said this: "When you have worked with the dead or the dying, you get a different philosophy about 'living'. I know how bad things can really get and you see families of the dying or the dead on the worst day of their lives. Once you have experienced that, other issues or situations in life are really put into **perspective**. That is why regardless of whether I play well or poorly, I just enjoy the whole experience of being here."

Because George had experienced and seen so many times how sad life can really be, he was the perfect person to be able to say that everything needs to be put into perspective, so we can just appreciate what we have. Those experiences that should be enjoyable need to be appreciated for what they are – enjoyable experiences! And experiences that cause stress or angst should be viewed with respect to the realities of life.

That round of golf when I caddied for George had a big impact on me because it made me realize that this is a philosophy that every entrepreneur needs to foster, develop and apply to everything they do as they go forward – try to get everything in your life into perspective.

## GETTING THINGS INTO PERSPECTIVE

Out of all the challenges you will face as an entrepreneur, getting things into perspective will be one of the hardest. If you are just about to embark on a new career as an entrepreneur or if you are already running your own business or social enterprise, then you will know how stressful some days can be. You will face a wide range of challenges – cash-flow problems, investment requirements, new sales opportunities, unhappy customers, demanding customers and staff issues, to name a few. This stress will manifest itself in a number of ways that could affect your relationships with your family, staff and customers, and critically your health.

Now, as I said in the introduction to this book, my stroke was caused by a deep vein thrombosis (a blood clot) that formed in my leg when I was flying to Boston for business. A bit of the clot broke off from a deep vein in my leg and travelled to my heart, where, unbeknown to me, I had a hole! The clot went through that hole and travelled to my brain, causing the stroke.

However, the months before the stroke, in 2006, were a very stressful time for me as a CEO. The company was having some serious staffing challenges and because of the economic climate, numerous customers had decided to hold back on any serious investments in web technology until the following year. In addition, we were in a dispute with one of our major suppliers. From a health perspective, I was not exercising and I was overweight.

Now, I don't know whether any of these factors contributed in any way to my stroke, but what I do know is that I was incredibly stressed. In hindsight, looking back on that time, what I was doing could not have been good for my health. And do you know something funny? The things I was stressed about were all resolved positively, and 11 years on the company is thriving. If I had only got into the habit of getting things in perspective back then – accepting that good and challenging issues would always present themselves to me as an entrepreneur – then I probably would not have been so stressed. Would that have prevented my stroke? Probably not, but it would have made my life – and the lives of my staff, clients and family – far more enjoyable. If only I had spent time with George and heard what he was facing every day – seeing families on the worst day of their lives – I might have been a bit more like him: calmer, enjoying the challenges I was facing and realizing that I was incredibly fortunate to be an entrepreneur.

So, don't underestimate the power of stress on the body and the mind as you go forward as an entrepreneur. Trying to keep things in perspective, even when you feel your head is going to explode, is crucial for success. There is a fine line between the adrenalin that drives you forward to achieve goals and the adrenalin that leads to stress and anxiety. Over the years I have crossed that line too many times and my relationships and my health have suffered. I have also made poor business decisions because I have got things way out of perspective – things that seemed critical at the time turned out to be not as bad as I had initially thought. Meetings I was dreading worked out fine. Pessimistic forecasts about the business never materialized. Yes, there were many days when things did not go to plan – when the company struggled, we lost business we should have won and clients were unhappy. But, because of the stress I felt I was under, and not getting things into perspective about how lucky and fortunate I actually was to be running my own business, I made bad decisions.

But, as you know, it is much easier to say "Get things into perspective" than to actually do it. So, how do you keep things in perspective so that you can cope with all the challenges you might face and, at the same time, enjoy your life as an entrepreneur?

## EXERCISE!

Well, I have found that the number-one thing any entrepreneur can do to help get things into perspective is to exercise regularly. I am not suggesting that you need to exercise like you are planning to run a marathon, but that you put at least four exercise sessions into your diary at the start of your week. Each one might be a session in the gym or a cycle ride or just a long, fast walk.

Whatever they are, you should see these sessions as the most important meetings you have in the week – more important than any client meeting!

The single biggest reason entrepreneurs should do this is to help improve their ability to focus. Exercise has positive effects on your brain, your energy levels and your mood, which all contribute to greater focus and productivity. You see, exercising increases your heart rate and gets more blood travelling around your body – and, crucially, to your brain. In addition, working out causes the body to produce serotonin, a natural anti-depressant. This can help significantly in managing stress levels. As every entrepreneur knows, mood can have a huge impact on focus, performance and decision making!

So, when you become more focused, energized and less stressed, you are more likely to keep things in perspective. When events turn to the worse, you are less likely to react irrationally or make rash decisions. Rather, you will be more objective and take time to talk to people you trust who will see the bigger picture, which can all help you to keep the situation in perspective.

For me, exercise is the most important thing an entrepreneur can do to help them keep perspective in their life. I cannot guarantee that you will have the same philosophy as George when I caddied for him, but I do know that scheduling a minimum of four 'meetings at the gym' every week will definitely help.

# 15.
# DRIVE

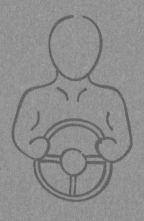

## THE PARADOX

# WHY WILL YOU NOT BE SATISFIED?

I have to say that one of the most enjoyable things I have ever done was writing my first book, *Changing Course*. Nobody was more surprised than me, firstly that I was able to write the book and then that I was able to secure a publishing deal. Not only did I enjoy the process of coming up with ideas, structuring them and then writing the book, I also loved the whole process of being involved in the publishing world and then launching the book with lots of press interviews, conferences to speak at and book festivals to attend.

However, the most rewarding aspect of the whole process is the feedback I receive from people who read my book. Some people have contacted me to ask whether I would meet them and provide them with advice on changing course, which I have been happy to do. Some have asked me to coach them to find their 'next thing'. And that is how I met Sarah.

Sarah had contacted me, via email, explaining how much she had enjoyed the book. She told me that she lived in Edinburgh and asked me whether we could meet since she had found my book so helpful. Two weeks later, I met Sarah for the first time.

Sarah was 45 and was having a career break at the time. Six months earlier she had sold her software consultancy business, a company she had founded ten years previously, and now she was looking for the next thing she could get her teeth into. We talked for an hour or so and we got on really well, to the extent that near the end of our meeting Sarah asked me whether

I would 'officially' coach her on a regular basis as she tried to work out what she should do next in her business life, which I was delighted to do.

I really enjoyed my time with Sarah. She was relaxed and thoughtful, and we had many fascinating and interesting meetings. However, it became very apparent that Sarah was not satisfied with what she had achieved in her business life. Initially I found this strange, for here was a person in her mid-forties who had tasted success more than once (she had sold another software company in 2005), had enough money in her bank account to never need to work again and could choose what she wanted to do with her life. But, the more we talked, the more I realized that she genuinely was not satisfied with what she had achieved. She was certainly not bored or lacking purpose, but she was not satisfied. So, in one of our sessions we talked in detail about this lack of satisfaction in her business life, and I asked her whether this troubled her.

She said, "There lies the paradox, that in searching for satisfaction you find that this is what **drives** you in business, but you never achieve that satisfaction. You are desperate to achieve it, but you just don't get it. So, you try and do something else that you are successful in, but you are still not satisfied. And round and round you go! Years ago, that did frustrate me, but now I see it as the main factor that makes me successful!"

Now, I don't know who got more out of that session but I certainly learnt a vital lesson on entrepreneurship – lacking a feeling of satisfaction in your business life is one of the main drivers that will make you successful.

# SEARCHING FOR SATISFACTION

Looking back on my own entrepreneurial life, I realized that a lack of satisfaction had actually been a positive thing. I have always been ambitious and enjoyed the buzz and excitement of trying to achieve success. Yes, I've had difficult and challenging times, but I have never been bored. And, when I did taste success, I did feel satisfied for a while. But, as Sarah explained so well, that feeling started to fade quickly, and I was driven to get involved in new things, as I wanted to feel satisfied again.

Since that insight from Sarah, I have chatted with several successful entrepreneurs, and I have found a common denominator in what drives all of them. No matter how successful they have become, they are always looking for the next project or business to get involved with. I know entrepreneurs who have built up large recruitment companies, sold them for a lot of money and then one year later founded a new recruitment company and started the whole process over again. I have seen very successful technology entrepreneurs who have made a fortune but then chosen to start a new technology company. And I have coached and worked with several CEOs whose balance sheets showed very large cash deposits in their bank account (meaning that if they got no more new business at all the company could still survive for two more years), but who were still driven to get more and more business.

When I talk to these people, they all share the same thing – they are not satisfied with what they have achieved so far in business. They all think that the next company or the next deal will finally give them the feeling of satisfaction they crave. But they eventually discover that it doesn't, and so off they go again.

A successful entrepreneur knows that satisfaction is what drives them, as they are constantly trying to achieve it. Striving for satisfaction means that you have a clear purpose, a belief in what you do, a vision that you stick to and plans that you are excited to carry out every day. That is why searching for satisfaction will make you successful as an entrepreneur. It is one of the main things that will make you driven in everything you do.

## THE PITBULL

Even though I have lived in Scotland for well over 30 years, I still support England when it comes to rugby. When I was growing up, one of my heroes in rugby was Brian Moore, an English hooker who was capped 64 times between 1987 and 1995 and went on two British and Irish Lions tours, winning five test caps. As a rugby player, his nickname was 'Pitbull' because of his attitude of never wanting to give up. He was loved by his teammates, and he was feared by the opposition. For me, though, he was one of the best players of his generation.

So, in 2012, I was delighted to hear him being interviewed on the radio about his life and the book he had just published. The interview covered most aspects of his life. He had been adopted when he was very young, found a real purpose in playing rugby in his teens, studied law at the University of Nottingham and became a solicitor. His rugby career was superb. He seemed to be very successful in everything he did. The interview was excellent and I learned a lot about him. The stand-out part for me was when he said he had been 'driven' in everything he had done in his life, but that he did not see himself as successful. He then went on to explain what he thought being driven is all about:

*You can be super-ambitious, but still not be driven.*
*Because super-ambitious people set their own goals,*
*and when they get there they are happy with them. Driven*
*people are not happy. They think they will become happy*
*because they think, "if I just get that or I just achieve that,*
*then I'll be fine."' And when they get there they find it is not*
*what they thought it would be and there is something else.*

Moore explained that he was not satisfied with what he had achieved in his life. For a while he would get some satisfaction from something he had done, but then a sabotage mechanism would hit in and his satisfaction would wane so that he was driven to find the next thing that, he hoped, would top up his feeling of satisfaction again.

For me, that describes in a nutshell what satisfaction, or lack of it, is. It is about being driven, not ambitious. Being ambitious is easy, but being driven is difficult because it takes a lot of energy, commitment and sacrifice to achieve something. Crucially, at the end of the day, when you get there, you know that you might feel satisfied for a while, but it will end. So you will be driven to move on as a new thing surfaces, and for a while that will motivate you like nothing else.

If you can recognize all of this and accept that it is an integral part of you, then use it, value it and be grateful that you have it, as it will help you in so many ways in your journey as an entrepreneur.

# 16.
# PEACE

# THE SEARCHING
# VENTURE CAPITALIST

# WHY DO YOU NEED TO FIND INNER PEACE?

My days of partying into the early hours of the morning have long gone. Yes, I might have a few beers in the pub with friends, but my age has finally caught up with me, and my days of partying are fortunately gone.

Mike from New York was 36 when we met, and his partying days were still in full swing!

Mike was playing with two friends, who also were from New York and had just arrived in Scotland that morning. It was agreed on the first tee that Mike would go first. I have witnessed countless drives from the first tee, but I have to say that Mike's was undoubtedly one of the worst! He just about managed to connect with the ball, hitting it with the toe of the club. The ball ran left, bouncing down the steps to the professional shop, ending up in the doorway. Not a great start to the round!

"Brilliant shot, Mike, one of your best," said one of his friends before falling about laughing.

"I knew I shouldn't have played golf today," he replied, also laughing. "Partying heavily in Greece for a week and then playing golf on the day we arrive is obviously not a great mix!"

Over the next few holes, Mike told me that he was currently a private investor in several technology companies. In a previous life, he'd been a very successful stock market trader for nine years on the New York Stock Exchange. However, the stress, the pressure and the lifestyle had finally become too much.

"It's a young person's game," he told me.

So he quit, and rather than working for someone else, he started making investments in technology companies using the experience he had gained as a trader. He made a number of investments and then hit gold two years later by investing in a new social media app. The initial investment he made increased over 15 times, and he had been able to cash in a few months ago.

"Wow, with that type of success my guess is that nothing keeps you awake at night," I said. "You have financial security, are your own boss and have control of your diary."

"Absolutely, but there is one thing that keeps me awake," he replied. "Boredom and lack of direction in my life."

I hadn't seen that coming! Mike told me how he missed the buzz of being a trader, working in a team and experiencing the ups and downs of doing deals. He wanted to find his identity again. Over the past six months, he had tried to do that by travelling and partying across Europe. That was why he had gone to Greece the week before. He'd been partying every night and, although it had been great fun, he still felt directionless and bored. He told me that he had found material success but not what he called 'inner **peace**'.

As we played the last few holes, I reflected on what Mike had shared with me. Here was a very successful person who had made a significant amount of money; could travel anywhere in the world; and could stay in the best hotels and party, eat and drink as much as he wanted. But, at the end of the day, he was bored and had no direction. As Mike said, he craved 'inner peace', and that for me is crucial for a successful entrepreneur. However you measure success – financial, material, work, personal – the phrase 'inner peace' is fundamental.

## MAKING PEACE WITH YOURSELF

Over the years, I have met many successful entrepreneurs. Well, on paper they seem successful – large bank balances, nice cars, big houses, holiday homes. And they come across as confident, self-assured and in control of their lives. But I wonder how many are like Mike. On the surface, life could not be better, but scratch a little bit below the surface, and everything is not what it seems. How many are bored, lacking direction, or slightly agitated and restlessness?

To help ease that boredom and restlessness, some might become angel investors, investing in new start-up companies and sharing their own experiences and their money. Because they have been successful once, they want to do it again. But for some reason, they don't find the 'buzz' and excitement they expected. Others decide to travel, party and take long holidays. At the start, this seems to be a great lifestyle, but over time both the body and mind become bored and restless. Some people decide they want to give something back and volunteer their time for a social enterprise or a charity. Again, same outcome. And they just cannot pin down why they are not at peace with themselves.

Now, I am not saying all successful entrepreneurs feel like that. On the contrary, there will be many who achieve material success and inner peace. But there will also be many like Mike who are not at peace with themselves no matter what material success they achieve.

So, as you embark on your own entrepreneurial course, or if you are three quarters of the way along it already, how do you avoid the feelings of discontentment that Mike and many other entrepreneurs suffer? In other words, how do you achieve material success and at the same time find inner peace?

## BEER WITH IMPACT AND PURPOSE

Well, let me tell you about a brilliant business based in Scotland called BrewDog, which produces and sells craft beers. The company was formed in 2007 by James Watt and Martin Dickie. In 2007 they had two employees, whereas today they employ well over 750 people, sell their beer around the world and have 46 bars. They have fantastic products with a variety of wonderful names – Punk IPA, Cocoa Psycho and Elvis Juice, to name a few. In 2009, they launched an investment scheme called Equity for Punks. In a groundbreaking first, they offered people the opportunity to buy shares in their company online. Over 1,300 invested and their 'anti-business' business model was born. Today they have over 57,000 Equity Punks.

In 2017, Watt and Dickie did an extraordinary thing, something that most businesses – small or large – do not do. They made a public statement that from August of that year they were committed to giving away 20% of their profits, every single year. They do this through their BrewDog Unicorn Fund (launched in 2016). Half of the 20% is shared evenly with their entire team and the other half is donated to charities directly chosen by their team members and by the Equity Punk community. This fund is central to their business, and they want to use craft beer to make the world a better place for everyone.

In their press release that announced all of this, among many other things, Watt and Dickie said this:

*At BrewDog, we want to make the best beer on the planet, and we want to build a radical new type of business: a business that all of our amazing team members and all of our fantastic Equity Punks are proud to be a part of.*

*This is not about altruism. It is about impact.*

*This is not about profits. It is about purpose.*

How powerful are those two last lines?

Now, I have no idea whether Watt and Dickie sleep well at night. My guess is they might, because on paper they have achieved material entrepreneurial success, but that alone does not seem to be what drives them. They seem to want to make an impact not only on the lives of their staff and their Equity Punks, but also on the wider world. By doing that, they might have got the inner peace that Mike was searching for, because they have found that it is not all about profits and looking after yourself – entrepreneurship can give you real inner peace, as you can make a direct positive impact on many people.

So, impact and purpose make for a very powerful combination to help you find inner peace. Don't give your time to a social enterprise just because you want to give something back. Do it because you really believe in its purpose and because you feel you can really help the enterprise to make an impact. Don't invest in an enterprise simply because you might get a great return. Ensure its purpose aligns with your values and principles, and work with it knowing that you can impact its business in a positive way. Yes, you can travel and party for a while, but that alone will not give you the satisfaction you are craving.

Look at Mike, bored of partying, travelling and making lots of money. He was searching for that missing thing in his life – this inner peace. But my hunch is that if he continues to search for those material things, then he will never find it. He also needs to search for the things that give him a real purpose – areas where he knows he will make a positive impact in his own life and the lives of those around him.

Take lessons from the guys at BrewDog and try to combine material and financial success with purpose and impact. If you do that, then there is a good chance you will find the inner peace for which so many entrepreneurs are searching.

# 17.
# PERSEVERANCE

## CHALLENGE
## THE IMPOSSIBLE

# WHY WILL IT BE TOUGH?

Sometimes you read a newspaper article or a blog, or watch TV, and you marvel at someone else's achievements. Then, a few years later, that same person comes to your attention again, having achieved something even bigger, and you are nearly speechless with admiration. Well, that happened to me when I saw that Mark Beaumont had reclaimed the world record for circumnavigating the globe by bike, by doing it in only 79 days. He had been inspired by Jules Verne's classic novel *Around the World in Eighty Days.*

Beaumont set off from the Arc de Triomphe, in Paris, on 2 July 2017 and he arrived back in Paris on 18 September 2017. He had cycled through Europe, Russia, Mongolia, China, Australia, New Zealand and North America. In total, he had covered 18,000 miles, which meant that he had completed 240 miles a day, spending 16 hours each day in the saddle.

I have to admit that Beaumont has been one of my heroes since 2008, when I watched the BBC documentary *The Man Who Cycled the World*, which charted his first successful attempt to cycle around the world (which he did in 194 days).

I watched a good piece on the BBC Evening News about Beaumont's achievement, but the bit that really stood out for me was when he said this:

*This has been, without doubt, the most punishing challenge
I have ever put my body and mind through. The physical and
mental stamina required for each day was a challenge in itself.*

With this statement fresh in my mind and having recently had a thought-provoking conversation with a close friend, Simon Duffy, I realized that I needed to include this very important fundamental of entrepreneurship, **perseverance**, in this book. In fact, not only does Beaumont embody perseverance in everything he does, but so does Simon.

Simon and I were at school together and after school, in 1983, he went to the University of Edinburgh to study for a degree in Politics and Philosophy. I went to Kirkcaldy College of Technology to do a Higher National Diploma in Communication Studies – at the opposite end of the education spectrum! I then moved to Edinburgh, where I shared a flat with Simon for a short while. He went on to do a PhD and I went off to sell life insurance! Simon met his wife, Nicola, at my wedding and I am the godfather of his son, a duty I carry out very poorly! He is, without question, one of my closest friends.

Over the past 35 years, I have witnessed Simon grow and develop into a great entrepreneur. What I admire most about Simon is that he is not driven by status, money or material goods. He has a belief and a passion to help people on the edge of society – the poor, the disadvantaged and people with learning disabilities. Simon has committed his adult life to this mission.

Simon believes that, in the main, the state and, to some extent, society at large, fail to understand and care for these people on the margins, and therefore the support they offer and provide is fundamentally flawed. So, like any good entrepreneur, over the years Simon has set up several organizations that directly support these people. Simon has helped thousands of people, published many books and articles on social justice, and spoken at conferences and events around the world.

In 2009, Simon and Nicola set up the Centre for Welfare Reform. From a standing start, they have built an organization that today is giving a voice to the poor, the disadvantaged and people with learning disabilities. The centre does this by running events, publishing papers and books, and campaigning and lobbying politicians and other people in power. Today it has over 900 publications in its online library, has over 80 fellows who believe and share in the same principles and values, and is regularly running events and campaigning against injustice in society. But achieving all of this has not been easy. The centre is challenging the status quo on how the state and the government support and care for the most vulnerable in society. Taking on the government not only requires a belief that what you are doing is correct, but also demands a lot of perseverance, and the centre constantly encounters barriers in trying to get its messages and publications out to wider sections of the population.

Nowadays Simon and I see each other less often than we used to, but we catch up through regular phone calls. In fact, we spoke on the phone the day that I watched the Mark Beaumont interview. Among many things we talked about, Simon told me how the Centre for Welfare Reform was doing, saying that there were tough days when he seemed to take one step forward, but then go three steps back. Then there were days when he felt he was making significant progress and just getting positive feedback from the people he was helping made it all worthwhile.

He said, "Do you know something, Neil, what I am trying to achieve – a world where everyone matters – might seem to be impossible, but I see it as an adventure and, as in all adventures, there will be tough times, fun times, difficult times and exciting times. But I know what my goal is and it gives me purpose."

That for me is perseverance in a nutshell – sticking with your overall goal and purpose, just as Mark Beaumont demonstrated so well!

## NEVER GIVE UP

Entrepreneurship can come with a lot of challenges and obstacles, whether you are a solo entrepreneur or running a large company. So, don't let anyone kid you – it can be tough. Entrepreneurship is not as glamorous as it seems. Yes, at the start it is about ideas, hopes and dreams, but it also requires guts and determination. It is about constantly trying to do things better, to innovate. If you view it as a way to gain fame and fortune, think again.

At the end of the day, entrepreneurship is a game of attrition, where perseverance is key. It is about discipline, routine and working incredibly hard. It is about sticking to your principles and values. And it is about keeping going no matter how tough it gets. And that needs perseverance!

Don't think for a moment that the famous entrepreneurs who are always used as examples of success had it easy. Karren Brady, Richard Branson, Sergey Brin, Bill Gates, Arianna Huffington, Steve Jobs, Larry Page and Mark Zuckerberg, to name a few, all had to work incredibly hard, make huge sacrifices and persevere day in, day out, no matter how difficult things became.

Today in the UK alone, even though they are not household names, hundreds of thousands of entrepreneurs are persevering towards what they believe in and what they are trying to achieve. They have the vision to see what others don't, the passion to motivate themselves and their staff, the purpose that drives them to get out of bed in the morning, the skill to build and grow a business, and the guts to make difficult decisions. But the glue that binds these ingredients together is the perseverance to stick with it day in, day out, year after year.

So yes, it is tough, but it is also incredibly rewarding when you have persevered, sacrificed, toiled and never given up. When success does occur, you know that you really deserve it in whatever form it takes. So, enjoy success when it happens because you know that the next day, the next week or the next year there will new challenges and obstacles to overcome. Perseverance is a truly great attribute to have in an entrepreneur's armoury.

## STROKE LESSONS

I am one of the countless entrepreneurs who can look back and remember how difficult it was at times. Examples include clients for whom we had worked for many years calling to say their budgets had been cut and cancelling the project we had planned; our bank being unable to extend our overdraft because of the credit crunch; and a key and senior part of my leadership team resigning and joining one of our competitors. In situations like these and countless others, my team and I had to persevere if we had any chance of getting through the difficult times.

Since 2009, I have been involved with many businesses, either as a consultant or as a director. I have witnessed, first hand, the tough and challenging decisions that have been made in order for businesses to survive. I have sat in board meetings where it was agreed that the business would need to make redundancies. I have seen senior staff lending significant amounts of money to the business so that all the staff could get paid at the end of the month. I have had one-to-one discussions with CEOs who told me that the stress they were under was significantly affecting their families. But many have got through these times – because they persevered.

The principal lesson I learned from my stroke concerned perseverance. From very early on, I realized that if I was going to achieve anything worthwhile after my stroke, I would have to stick with it. You see, when you have a stroke, the doctors tell you that you will make the most progress in the first six to nine months. Then progress starts to plateau and after a year or so it really levels out, and you are unlikely to make any more significant improvement. That indeed was my experience. The weeks and months after my stroke, my memory, speech, tiredness and logical thinking were terrible. With help from my doctors and family, and crucially with time, I started to make slow but steady progress. Although my speech, memory, tiredness and logical thinking had all improved after about 18 to 24 months, I knew I would have some permanent damage in these areas. So, I eventually concluded that I needed to accept my lot and move on despite the many challenges ahead. My recovery was an exercise of perseverance. It took a long time and I shed many tears, had huge mood swings and became incredibly frustrated and anxious. But, with the support of my medical team, friends and family, I kept persevering.

After two years, when I tried to go back to work, it was very difficult. At first, I was embarrassed when I kept losing words and was not able to explain things well. However, I knew I had to keep putting myself out there and meet new people. I also soon realized that there were some things I simply could not do any longer. So, I had to learn to let these go and focus on the things I could still do well.

Today, as I look back to 19 October 2006 when I had my stroke, I can see that I have come a long way. During this time, I have had fantastic support from so many people, which has allowed me to find a new way forward. And, although I wish my stroke had not happened, I can now see lots of positive things that have come from it. I doubt very much that I would have written two books, become a caddie, helped my son set up his own business, got involved with a variety of businesses, and met some great and inspirational people if I had not had my stroke. These, and many other things, I see today as positive outcomes.

So, take heart from Mark Beaumont, Simon Duffy, myself and countless numbers of other people who have weathered difficult and challenging situations: see your goal in whatever you do as an adventure, with perseverance driving you ever closer to achieving it.

# 18.
# PERSONAL

IT'S YOUR BABY

# WHY WILL YOU GET HURT?

One of the biggest challenges you will face as an entrepreneur is when the time comes to decide whether to sell the business you founded, let someone else run it or continue to stay in control.

At the beginning, as an entrepreneur you are convinced that it is only you who can lead your start-up to huge success. When you start off as an entrepreneur, your business idea is normally just that – an idea only. You are the person who has the belief, desire and vision to build a great business from your initial idea. It is you who can see the opportunity that your innovative product or service will provide, and you are determined to capitalize on it. So, you go for it and secure the finance you need to start the business. If it looks like things are going well, then you hire the people to help build the business according to your vision, and you develop close relationships with those first employees. You might take on the role of the CEO, but not always. Whatever your role is, you create the culture of the business, which normally is an extension of your personality, and you set the agenda. From the start, employees, customers and suppliers identify your business with you, the founder. You then start to have some success and your business grows.

Very quickly this whole process becomes very **personal** – you feel that you have created a business, nurtured it and helped it grow. New ventures are usually labours of love for entrepreneurs, and they become emotionally attached to them, sometimes referring to the business as 'my baby' or using similar parenting language without even noticing.

So, because things are going well and you want to see your 'baby' grow, you might decide to pursue or accept investments or a loan in order to expand your business by way of employing more staff, investing in new technology or moving to bigger offices. In doing so, you relinquish some control and shares of the business you founded to a board of directors. If things are going well, you will be left alone to run the business without lots of interference from the board.

However, if you are underperforming, the board will ask for a change in the way you run things. This might involve forcing you to bring new faces into the leadership team or, worse, it might force you to give up the role of CEO and bring in someone the board thinks will take the business to the next level. For an entrepreneur (the founder), this can be a very difficult time – you either take on another (less senior) position or you leave.

These types of scenarios can be very emotional. It might seem a strange thing to say, but when you have founded a business, grown it, employed some brilliant people and built relationships with clients, it becomes like family – a big part of you. And, as if it were part of your family, if it gets hurt or is unjustly criticized, you take it personally and get very emotional.

## IT IS PERSONAL

Feeling so involved in your business can bring lots of benefits; however, it can also bring you some of the most difficult of challenges. As an entrepreneur, you will become very protective of the business you have founded. If anyone tries to harm your business deliberately, then you will become incredibly angry and upset about it. For example, if you find that someone, maybe an old client or competitor, has said unjust or unfounded things about any aspect of your business, you are likely to take it very personally. You will see any attack on the business as a personal attack on you. Other directors and staff who were not there at the very start, when the business was only an idea, will not have the same level of emotional investment in it. Yes, they will care and they will be concerned, but in a different way. You see your business as a big part of you and your life. And it really hurts when someone wrongly criticizes it.

This doesn't only apply to start-ups. After my stroke, when I was unable to continue as a CEO, the Finance Director at the time, Andy, took over my role as CEO. It was a very difficult time for everyone. Not only did Andy need to take on the new responsibilities that came with the CEO role, but this was also at the beginning of the credit crunch and our bank, without any notice, removed our overdraft. To get through this difficult period, Andy re-mortgaged his house and lent a significant amount of money to the business. Most of the directors lent money too, but nowhere near the same amount as Andy. Andy now rightly owns the majority of the shares because he took the biggest risk to keep the business afloat. Since he became the CEO, Andy and I have had many conversations where he has been immensely angry or upset about an unjust or unfounded situation that has threated the business. Reflecting back on those conversations I had with Andy made me realize that when I was the CEO, I also saw any attack on the business as a personal attack – it hurt because I was so emotionally invested in the business. Even now, although I stopped being the CEO 11 years ago, I still feel hurt and angry when the business comes under false attack!

Equally, when someone comes knocking on your door wanting to buy your business, that can also be a difficult and painful process to go through. Yes, the obvious upsides are mainly financial: don't underestimate them, and enjoy and celebrate when that happens. But understand that selling your business – letting go of everything you have built – can be a real challenge and you will feel a degree of pain when it happens. I went through this process as a CEO when we sold the company to a major client of ours. Yes, we did a good deal, and I was financially far better off. But, if I am honest, there was a significant degree of sadness when I sold the majority of my shares and gave up control of my 'baby'.

Now, the following is a very important aspect of entrepreneurship: *if you don't identify with what I've been talking about, if you don't feel that high level of emotional investment, then perhaps you don't care enough, and it is time to do something else. Not only are you kidding yourself, but you are also not being fair to your staff, clients, investors and shareholders.*

## GREAT NEWS

So, as an entrepreneur, you really do need to feel the hurt – it is critical for your business. If you get that feeling or can imagine the hurt, then for me you have understood and live by one of the most important fundamentals an entrepreneur requires to be successful – you really care, value and love what you do. Consequently, you will do anything to protect your business, like you would protect your family. During difficult times, you will be driven, like no one else in your business, to solve the problems you are facing. You will surprise yourself by how innovative and 'out of the box' your thinking will become, and you will become even more energized and motivated to make things work.

The great news is that it works both ways. You will experience enjoyment and pride when good things happen to your business. Maybe you will bump into an old employee who tells you that they really enjoyed working for you. Or a client calls to say they are delighted with the work you've just done for them. Or you get an email from a potential new client saying that your company has been recommended to do a project for them. All this will give you an immense feeling of satisfaction.

## THE ENTREPRENEUR'S BOOK

As an entrepreneur, I realize I am in an incredibly privileged position. Not only can I decide *what* I will do with my time, but I can also decide *why* I will do it. And I have learned this not only from books, courses and TED Talks, but also from meeting a wide range of wise and inspirational people and listening to their stories and experiences. Some of these people are in this book, and I hope you enjoyed meeting them!

Today, as I sit in my office writing this final chapter, I can see that what I do as an entrepreneur has been shaped by answering the 'why' questions that I have shared in this book. I still enjoy caddying and I continue to do it, as the people I meet **inspire** me. I still love being involved in the business I started over 20 years ago, and I feel incredibly **proud** of all it has achieved. Helping my son set up a digital agency, watching it starting to grow and develop, and now being its chairman is a huge **honour** for me. And being an author, which allows me to share my thoughts

and ideas with a wider audience, **motivates** me. This is my entrepreneurial life today, and it is not a bad life at all!

These feelings of inspiration, pride, honour and motivation have
come from understanding and acting on these 'why' questions.
Through these questions, I have found what the core fundamentals
of successful entrepreneurship consist of: belief, purpose, values,
desire, love, morals, ownership, compassion, luck, failure, trust,
copying, loneliness, perspective, drive, peace and perseverance.

It has taken me a long time to understand all of these, and I have
made many mistakes along the way – and I will continue to make
mistakes! But I have found that, once I understood and applied
the core fundamentals, my own entrepreneurial journey became
far more rewarding, fulfilling and enjoyable. I am proud to be one
of the many successful entrepreneurs who believe there is purpose, value and meaning in what they do.

At the end of the day, I am not an entrepreneur because I want
wealth, status or recognition, but because it is personal, and I just
love it!

# INSPIRING AND BRILLIANT INDIVIDUALS AND COMPANIES THAT APPEAR IN THIS BOOK

**CHAPTER 1**

Ikirezi Natural Products, https://www.ikirezi.com

**CHAPTER 2**

Dan Buettner, "How to Live to Be 100+," TED Talk,
    September 2009, https://www.ted.com/talks/dan_buettner_
    how_to_live_to_be_100
Tom Hanks interviewed on *Desert Island Discs*, BBC Radio 4,
    13 May 2016, http://www.bbc.co.uk/programmes/b079m78n

**CHAPTER 3**

Buffer, "The 10 Buffer Values and How We Act on Them Every Day,"
    7 January 2015, https://open.buffer.com/buffer-values

**CHAPTER 4**

Barefoot Sanctuary,
    http://www.barefootambition.co.uk

**CHAPTER 5**
Clarence Francis (1888-1985), Chairman of General Foods
"The Causes of Industrial Peace," speech, National Association
    of Manufacturers, 4 December 1947
Value The Person International, http://www.valuetheperson.com
Gallup, *State of the American Workplace*, 2013
Gallup Q12, https://q12.gallup.com

**CHAPTER 6**
*The Apprentice*,
    https://en.wikipedia.org/wiki/The_Apprentice_(UK_TV_series)

**CHAPTER 7**
Cyndi Crother, *Catch!: A Fishmonger's Guide to Greatness*,
    Berrett-Koehler Publishers, 10 January 2005
Pike Place Fish Market, https://www.pikeplacefish.com

**CHAPTER 8**
Sporting Memories, http://www.sportingmemoriesnetwork.com
Tim Minchin, "Occasional Address"
    (University of Western Australia), 25 September 2013,
    http://www.timminchin.com/2013/09/25/occasional-address

**CHAPTER 9**
Lisa Eadicicco, "One of Apple's Earliest Employees
    Describes the First Time Steve Jobs Met His Genius Cofounder
    Steve Wozniak," *Business Insider UK*, 8 December 2014,
    http://uk.businessinsider.com/how-steve-jobs-met-steve-
    wozniak-2014-12

Marguerite Ward, "Mark Zuckerberg Returns to the Harvard Dorm Room Where Facebook Was Born," *CNBC Make It*, 25 May 2017, https://www.cnbc.com/2017/05/25/mark-zuckerberg-returns-to-the-harvard-dorm-where-facebook-was-born.html

Chris Hughes, *Fair Shot: Rethinking Inequality and How We Earn*, Bloomsbury, 2018

Ed Conway, "Review: Fair Shot by Chris Hughes – Should We Listen to This Facebook Tech-Nerd?," *The Times Saturday Review*, 24 March 2018, https://www.thetimes.co.uk/article/review-fair-shot-by-chris-hughes-should-we-listen-to-this-facebook-tech-nerd-9m82jx7p8

## CHAPTER 10

Duncan Logan, https://www.rocketspace.com

J. K. Rowling, "Text of J. K. Rowling's Speech" (Harvard University), 5 June 2008, https://news.harvard.edu/gazette/story/2008/06/text-of-j-k-rowling-speech

## CHAPTER 11

Nick Freer, "Let's Give a Big Cheer to Two Big Ears," *The Scotsman*, 9 June 2016, https://www.scotsman.com/business/companies/tech/nick-freer-let-s-give-a-big-cheer-to-two-big-ears-1-4149271

Steve Jobs, "Steve's Jobs Stanford Commencement Speech," 12 June 2005, https://www.youtube.com/watch?v=D1R-jKKp3NA

Jean-Dominique Bauby, "The Diving-Bell and the Butterfly," HarperCollins Publishers; Film tie-in edition (7 May 2008)

*The Diving Bell and the Butterfly*, 2007. Production companies Pathe Renn Productions and France 3 Cinema

**CHAPTER 12**
Austin Kleon, *Steal Like an Artist*, Workman Publishing, 2012.
Jack Nicklaus, http://www.nicklaus.com/newsletter-2011/
  december/GD_Dec11_Flick.pdf

**CHAPTER 13**
John Rampton, "12 Organizations Entrepreneurs Need to Join,"
  *Entrepreneur*, 2 January 2015,
  https://www.entrepreneur.com/article/241192

**CHAPTER 15**
Brian Moore interviewed on *Desert Island Discs*, BBC Radio 4,
  2 March 2012, http://www.bbc.co.uk/programmes/b01cj4ky

**CHAPTER 16**
BrewDog, https://www.brewdog.com/about/culture

**CHAPTER 17**
Mark Beaumont, https://markbeaumontonline.com
Centre for Welfare Reform, http://www.centreforwelfarereform.org/
  about-us

# ABOUT THE AUTHOR

**NEIL FRANCIS** is an author, coach and the co-founder of Pogo Studio, a digital consultancy practice. He is also director of two internet companies and a social enterprise. Over the years, he has worked with hundreds of companies, from SMEs to global organizations, helping them to use digital technology effectively and creatively.

In 1996 he co-founded one of the first internet and web development companies in the UK. During that time, he sold the company to a major client and then two years later led the team that bought the company back. Neil worked as CEO for the company for 11 years, until he had a stroke in 2006 at aged 41. This forced him to change the direction of his life. To help with his recovery, he became a golf caddie. These experiences led him to write his first book, *Changing Course*, which was published in 2013 by Hay House. Neil lives in North Berwick with his family.

## CONTACT THE AUTHOR
**neil@neil-francis.com**
**www.neil-francis.com**

in linkedin.com/in/neil-francis-7a72118/
@neilfrancisauthor

# LID 25TH ANNIVERSARY

## Sharing knowledge since 1993

- 1993 Madrid
- 2008 Mexico DF and Monterrey
- 2010 London
- 2011 New York and Buenos Aires
- 2012 Bogotá
- 2014 Shanghai